Landlords' Rights & Duties in North Carolina

with forms

LANDLORDS' RIGHTS & DUTIES IN NORTH CAROLINA

with forms

Jacqueline D. Stanley
Mark Warda
Attorneys at Law

First Edition, 1999

Published by: **Sphinx® Publishing, A Division of Sourcebooks, Inc.®**

Naperville Office
P.O. Box 372
Naperville, Illinois 60566
630-961-3900
Fax: 630-961-2168

Clearwater Office
P.O. Box 25
Clearwater, Florida 33757
727-587-0999
Fax: 727-586-5088

Interior Design and Production: Amy S. Hall and Edward A. Haman, Sourcebooks, Inc.®

Library of Congress Cataloging-in-Publication Data

Stanley, Jacqueline D.
Landlords' Rights and Duties in North Carolina : with forms / Jacqueline D. Stanley & Mark Warda. -- 1st ed.
p. cm.
Includes index.
ISBN 1-57248-091-2 (pbk)
1. Landlord and tenant--North Carolina Popular works. 2. Landlord and tenant--North Carolina Forms. I. Warda, Mark. II. Title.
III. Title: Landlords' rights and duties in North Carolina.
KFN7517.Z9S85 1999
346.75604'34--dc21 99-35772
CIP

Printed and bound in the United States of America.

Paperback — 10 9 8 7 6 5 4 3 2 1

Contents

Using Self-Help Law Books

Whenever you shop for a product or service, you are faced with various levels of quality and price. In deciding what product or service to buy, you make a cost/value analysis on the basis of your willingness to pay and the quality you desire.

When buying a car, you decide whether you want transportation, comfort, status, or sex appeal. Accordingly, you decide among such choices as a Neon, a Lincoln, a Rolls Royce, or a Porsche. Before making a decision, you usually weigh the merits of each option against the cost.

When you get a headache, you can take a pain reliever (such as aspirin) or visit a medical specialist for a neurological examination. Given this choice, most people, of course, take a pain reliever, since it costs only pennies; whereas a medical examination costs hundreds of dollars and takes a lot of time. This is often the most logical choice: it's rare to need anything more than a pain reliever for a headache. But in some cases, a headache may indicate a brain tumor, and failing to see a specialist right away can result in complications. Should everyone with a headache go to a specialist? Of course not, but people treating their own illnesses must realize that they are betting on the basis of their cost/value analysis of the situation; they are taking the most logical option.

The same cost/value analysis must be made in deciding to do one's own legal work. Many legal situations are very straightforward, requiring a simple form and no complicated analysis. Anyone with a little intelligence and a book of instructions can handle the matter without outside help.

But there is always the chance that complications are involved that only an attorney would notice. To simplify the law into a book like this, several legal cases often must be condensed into a single sentence or paragraph. Otherwise, the book would be several hundred pages long and too complicated for most people. However, this simplification necessarily leaves out many details and nuances that would apply to special or unusual situations. Also, there are many ways to interpret most legal questions. Your case may come before a judge who disagrees with the analysis of our authors.

Therefore, in deciding to use a self-help law book and to do your own legal work, you must realize that you are making a cost/value analysis. You have decided that the money you will save in doing it yourself outweighs the chance your case will not turn out to your satisfaction. Most people handling their own simple legal matters never have a problem, but occasionally people find that it ended up costing them more to have an attorney straighten out the situation than it would have if they had hired an attorney in the beginning. Also, you may not be able to undo some mistakes. Keep this in mind while handling your case, and be sure to consult an attorney if you feel you might need further guidance.

Introduction

North Carolina's landlord/tenant laws are like a double-edged sword. If a landlord does not know about them, or ignores them, he or she can lose thousands of dollars in lost rent, penalties, and attorney's fees. However, a landlord who knows the law can use the procedures to simplify life and to save money. Knowledge is power and knowing the laws to governing rentals will give you the power to protect your rights and to deal with problems effectively.

Laws are written to be precise, not to be easily readable. This book explains the law in simple language so that North Carolina landlords can know what is required of them and know their rights under the law. If you would like more detail about a law, you can check the statutes in appendix A or research the court cases as explained in chapter 1.

This book includes the most recent statutory and case law changes as of the time of printing. However, you need to be aware that nearly every year the North Carolina legislature passes new laws regulating landlord/tenant relations, and the courts of the state write more opinions interpreting those laws and further defining the rights of landlords and tenants.

No book of this type can be expected to cover every situation that may arise. Laws change and different judges have different interpretations of what the laws mean. Only a lawyer, reviewing the unique characteristics of your situation, can give you an opinion of how the laws apply to your case. This book can give you the legal framework to avoid costly mistakes.

When following the procedures in this book it should be kept in mind that different counties have different customs and some judges have their own way of doing things, so the requirements in your area may differ somewhat from those outlined in this book. Clerks and judge's assistants cannot give you legal advice, but they can often tell you what they require in order to proceed with your case. Before filing any forms, ask if your court provides its own forms or has any special requirements.

1 Laws That Govern Rental Property

North Carolina Landlord/Tenant Law

North Carolina landlord/tenant law consists of both statutes passed by the legislature and legal opinions written by judges. The statutes usually address specific issues that have come up repeatedly in landlord/tenant relations. The judicial opinions interpret the statutes and decide what the law is in areas not specifically covered by statutes.

Unfortunately, since the statutes were written at different times by different legislators, they sometimes conflict. There are also regulations that conflict with those laws, and judges do not always interpret them in the same way. So a landlord can be caught in a "catch-22" situation where even an experienced lawyer cannot find an easy solution.

This is a rare situation. If it happens to you, your two choices are to fight the issue in a higher court or to give in and do what is demanded. Most small landlords cannot afford a long court battle, so the only practical solution is to relent. For this reason it is usually better to work out a settlement with a tenant than to let an issue go to a magistrate or before a judge. This will be explained in more detail later in the book.

Which North Carolina Laws Apply?

The laws governing landlords' rights and duties can be found in Chapter 42 of the North Carolina General Statutes, which includes the Tenant Security Deposit Act and the Residential Rental Agreement Act, as well as the laws governing the eviction of residential tenants and retaliatory evictions. Chapter 42 is divided into eight articles:

Article 1: General provisions.

Article 2: Agricultural Tenancies

Article 2A: Ejectment of Residential Tenants

Article 3: Summary Ejectment

Article 4A: Retaliatory Eviction

Article 5: Residential Rental Agreements

Article 6: Tenant Security Deposit Act

Article 7: Expedited Eviction of Drug Traffickers and Other Criminals

Applicability of Chapter 42

The laws outlined in Chapter 42 only apply to the landlord and tenant relationship. The landlord/tenant relationship is created through an agreement by the parties to the rental of real property. This agreement is commonly referred to as a *tenancy lease*. North Carolina law recognizes three types of leases. The differences may be subtle, but each type of lease has its own rights and duties. The laws outlined in Chapter 42 apply only to these type of relationships. The three types of leases are as follows:

Tenancy for Years

The distinguishing characteristic of a *tenancy for years* lease is that it has a fixed or definite term. A tenancy for years, despite the name, can last a week, a month, a year, or decade. This is the most common type of tenancy because there is no question as to when the agreement ends. In order to be valid, both parties must agree that the term or lease will expire on a specific date.

PERIODIC TENANCY

A *periodic tenancy* lease is one that is renewable at designated intervals, such as year-to-year, month-to-month, or week-to-week. Periodic tenancy's can arise through an agreement of the parties, but most often they are created at the end of a tenancy for years. For example, Larry Landlord and Tommy Tenant originally agree to a tenancy for years that will end on March 1, 2000. Tommy pays rent on a monthly basis. On March 1, 2000, Tommy stays and continues to pay rent each month. In this situation, the tenancy for years has been converted into periodic (month-to-month) tenancy.

TENANCY AT WILL

A *tenancy at will* is a lease agreement with no specific term. For example, Larry Landlord and Tommy Tenant agree that Tommy may lease his beach house until such time as Tommy grows tired of watching the waves come in or until Larry decides he needs it for weekly beach parties. A tenancy at will allows either party to terminate the agreement by simply giving the other party reasonable notice of their desire to end the tenancy. However, this type of tenancy agreement is a breeding ground for litigation, and is therefore not routinely used or recommended.

RENTALS COVERED BY CHAPTER 42

In addition to rentals of homes, duplexes, and apartments, the following types of rentals are, or at least may be, covered by Chapter 42:

Mobile Homes. Chapter 42 applies to mobile homes, both where the owner of the mobile home rents it to a tenant, and where a mobile home owner rents the landlord's space.

Boats. Boats could be covered under Chapter 42 if a magistrate determines that the boat constitutes a *dwelling*.

Commercial Tenancies. The provisions contained in Chapter 42 applies to commercial, as well as residential tenancies.

The following relationships are not considered to be a landlord and tenant relationship, and therefore, are not covered under Chapter 42:

RELATIONSHIPS NOT COVERED BY CHAPTER 42

Seller-Buyer. Sam Seller agreed to sell a home to Bill Buyer. Bill agreed to make monthly payments and is allowed to live in the home while making the payments. After a few months, Bill loses his job and is unable to make the payments. Sam wants Bill out of the dwelling. Sam can not use the provisions of Chapter 42 because he and Bill do not have a landlord/tenant relationship. It is a buyer-seller relationship. What if Sam and Bill had a landlord/tenant relationship prior to entering into the seller-buyer relationship? This would not be relevant unless the sales contract specifically states that if Bill breaches the contract, the parties will resume the landlord/tenant relationship.

Employer-Employee. Bob Boss owned a bed and breakfast, and hired Will Worker to serve as chef and host. Bob required Will to live on the premises. After a few months, they had a dispute and Bob fired Will and demanded that he leave the premises. Will refused to leave until his employment discrimination suit was mediated. Bob could not have Will removed under the provisions of Chapter 42. There is no landlord/tenant relationship because living on the premises was an essential aspect of Will's employment.

There are situations where an employer and employee can create a landlord/tenant relationship. For example, Larry owns rental houses, as well as a lumber company. One of Larry's employees in his lumber company needs an apartment. They enter into a rental agreement. This situation is a landlord/tenant relationship (it is not part employment) and Chapter 42 would apply.

Guests. Tommy Tenant invites Gina Girlfriend to live with him in the apartment he was leasing from Larry Landlord. They lived together and shared the rent. After three years, Tommy decided to move on to greener pastures and wanted Gina to leave. She refused. Could Tommy use Chapter 42 to have Gina removed? No, there is no landlord/tenant relationship between Tommy and Gina.

Hotels and Motels. Ivan Innkeeper owns a chain of motels. Greg Guest checks in for a weekend but refuses to leave on Monday morning. Ivan can not have him evicted under the provisions of Chapter 42. The line between innkeeper and guest and landlord and tenant is not always clear because some motels allow for extended stays and look a lot like efficiency apartments. In these instances, a magistrate will have to decide, based upon the facts, whether Chapter 42 would apply.

Nursing Homes. Chapter 42 does not apply to nursing homes. Laws governing nursing homes can be found at N.C.G.S. §§ 131E-115 to 131E-131.

Local Laws

In some areas, local governments have passed various rules regulating landlords. For example, in one county it could be a *crime* for a landlord not to have a walk-through inspection both before and after the tenancy, but this may not be a requirement in another county! Be sure to check with both your city and county governments for any local laws.

Federal Laws

Federal laws that apply to the rental of real estate include discrimination laws such as the Civil Rights Act, the Americans with Disabilities Act, and lead-based paint rules of the Environmental Protection Agency. These are explained in chapter 2 of this book.

The United States Department of Housing and Urban Development has a HUD handbook that explains the rules applicable to public housing and other HUD programs.

Doing Further Research

This book contains a summary of most of the significant court cases and statutes which affect landlord/tenant law in North Carolina. However, you may want to research your predicament further by reading the entire statute section or court case. To do this, you should use the statute section number or case citation. North Carolina Statute citations appear as "N.C.G.S. § 7A-216." North Carolina's landlord/tenant statutes are included in appendix A of this book.

Court cases are noted by the little book symbol: 🕮. Case citations include the name of the case, the volume and page of the reporter, and the court and year. For example, a citation for *Stone v. Guion*, 442 S.E.2d 94 (1994), means that the case titled *Stone v. Guion* is found in volume 442 of the *Southeastern Reporter, Second Series*, at page 94; and that it is a 1994 case. A North Carolina case citation might also appear as *Stone v. Guion*, 120 N.C. App. 552, 442 S.E. 2d 94 (1994). This means that the case can be found in volume 120 of the *North Carolina Reporter*, at page 552; or in the *Southeastern Reporter, Second Series*, as mentioned above.

To learn more about doing legal research you should refer to a book on the subject, such as *Legal Research Made Easy*, by Suzan Herskowitz, which is available from your local bookstore or directly from Sphinx Publishing by calling 1-800-226-5291.

Good Faith Obligation

Every residential agreement and duty under the landlord/tenant law requires *good faith*. The obligation to act in good faith is not a statutory requirement, however, it is an implied obligation. The failure to act in good faith, or engaging in conduct that could be construed as "dishonest, misleading, or fraudulent," could cause the court to rule against you, invalidate the rental agreement, and order you to pay attorney's fees. If the conduct is particularly offensive and found to be an "unfair trade practice," you could be ordered to pay punitive damages that are equal to three times the tenant's actual damages.

Fictitious Names

In North Carolina, as in most states, unless you do business in your own legal name, you must register the name you are using. Registrations of fictitious names are handled by each county.

You should be able to obtain the registration form from the Register of Deeds Office at the county courthouse. You should register the name in the county that will serve as your principal place of business.

There is an $8.00 filing fee. It is a misdemeanor to fail to register a fictitious name. If someone sues you and you are not registered, they may be entitled to attorney's fees and court costs.

If your name is John Doe, you may operate your business as "John Doe, Landlord," without registering it. But any other use of a name should be registered, such as:

Doe Realty	Doe Realty Company
Doe Company	N.C. Realty Company

You cannot use the words, "corporation," "incorporated," "corp.," or "inc.," unless you are a corporation. However, corporations do not have to register the name they are using unless it is different from their registered corporate name (N.C.G. S., Chapter 55-4-01).

When you use a fictitious name you are "doing business as" (abbreviated "d/b/a") whatever name you are using. For example: "John Doe d/b/a Doe Realty."

Creating the Landlord/Tenant Relationship

2

Screening Prospective Tenants

The first step in avoiding legal problems with tenants is to carefully choose who will be your tenant. As long as you do not discriminate based on such categories as race, sex, and age (see pages 14-19), you can be selective in to whom you rent your property. A tenant who has had the same apartment and job for the last five years will probably be a better risk than one who has been evicted several times.

You should get a written application from all prospective tenants. Besides allowing you to check their past record as a tenant, the information can be helpful in tracking them down if they disappear owing you rent or damages. (See form 1.) Be sure that the form you use does not ask illegal questions such as "nationality."

You should check the defendant index of the court records (not just the "official records") of your county or the last county they lived in to see if they have ever been evicted or sued. It would also be wise to check the plaintiff index to see if they have sued a landlord. In some counties, these indexes are combined.

You should check with a prior landlord to see if he or she would rent to the prospective tenant again. Don't bother checking with their present landlord. He or she may lie just to get rid of them! And be sure the people you talk to are really landlords. Some tenants use friends to pose as previous landlords and lie for them.

There are some companies which, for a fee, will investigate tenants, including employment, previous landlords, court cases, and their own files of "bad tenants." Some landlords require a non-refundable application fee to cover such an investigation. For more information, check your phone book under Credit Reporting Agencies.

Discrimination

Since Congress passed the Civil Rights Act of 1968, it has been a federal crime for a landlord to discriminate in the rental or sale of property on the basis of race, religion, sex, or national origin. In addition, North Carolina passed its own anti-discrimination statute which makes such acts a state crime and adds the additional category of handicapped persons. In 1988, the United States Congress passed an amendment to the Civil Rights Act that bans discrimination against both the handicapped and families with children. Except for apartment complexes which fall into the special exceptions, all rentals must now allow children in all units.

Civil Rights Act of 1968

Under the Civil Rights Act of 1968 (42 USC 3601-17), any policy which has a discriminatory effect is illegal.

Penalty. A victim of discrimination under this section can file a civil suit, a HUD complaint, or request the U.S. Attorney General to prosecute. Damages can include actual losses and punitive damages of up to $1,000. Failure to attend a hearing or to produce records can subject you to up to a year in prison or a $1,000 fine.

Limitation. The complaint must be brought within 180 days.

Exemptions. This law does not apply to single family homes if the owner owns three or less units, if there is no more than one sale within twenty-four months, if the person does not own any interest in more than three at one time, and if no real estate agent or discriminatory advertisement is used. It also does not apply to a property that the owner lives in if it has four or less units.

COERCION OR INTIMIDATION. Where coercion or intimidation is used to effectuate discrimination, there is no limit to when the action can be brought or the amount of damages. For example, a real estate agent fired for renting to African-Americans. *Wilkey v. Pyramid Construction Co.*, 619 F.Supp. 1453 (D. Conn. 1983).

CIVIL RIGHTS ACT § 1982

The Civil Rights Act § 1982 (42 USC 1982) is similar to the above statute, but where the above law applies to any policy which has a discriminatory effect, this law applies only where it can be proved that the person had an intent to discriminate.

PENALTY. Actual damages plus unlimited punitive damages. In 1992, a jury in Washington, DC, awarded civil rights groups $850,000 damages against a developer who only used Caucasian models in rental advertising. *The Washington Post* now requires that the models in ads it accepts must be twenty-five percent African-America to reflect the percentage of African-American's in the Washington area.

LIMITATION. None.

EXEMPTIONS. None.

CIVIL RIGHTS ACT 1988 AMENDMENT

The 1988 Amendment to the Civil Rights Act (42 USC 3601) bans discrimination against the handicapped and families with children. Unless a property falls into one of the exemptions, it is illegal under this law to refuse to rent to persons because of age or to refuse to rent to children. While landlords may be justified in feeling that children cause damage to their property which they wish to avoid, Congress has ruled that the right of families to find housing is more important than the rights of landlords to protect the condition of their property. The exemptions are for two types of housing: 1) where the units are rented solely by persons sixty-two or older; or 2) where eighty percent of the units are rented to persons fifty-five or older. In late 1995, the law was amended so that the property does not need to have special facilities for such persons' needs.

Regarding the disabled, the law allows them to remodel the unit to suit their needs as long as they return it to the original condition upon leaving. It also requires new buildings of four units or more to have electrical facilities and common areas accessible to the disabled.

PENALTY. $10,000 for first offense, $25,000 for second violation within five years and up to $50,000 for three or more violations within seven years. Unlimited punitive damages in private actions.

LIMITATION. Complaint can be brought within two years for private actions.

EXEMPTIONS. This law does not apply to single family homes if the owner owns three or less units, if there is no more than one sale within twenty-four months, if the person does not own any interest in more than three at one time, and if no real estate agent or discriminatory advertisement is used. (A condominium unit is not a single-family home so is not exempt.) It also does not apply to a property that the owner lives in if it has four or less units. Additionally, there are exemptions for dwellings in state and federal programs for the elderly, for complexes that are solely used by persons sixty-two or older, and for complexes used solely by persons fifty-five or over if there are substantial facilities designed for the elderly, for religious housing, and for private clubs.

AMERICANS WITH DISABILITIES ACT

The Americans with Disabilities Act (ADA) requires that "reasonable accommodations" be made to provide the disabled with access to commerical premises and forbids discrimination against them. If any commercial premises are remodeled, the remodeling must include modifications that make the premises accessible. All new construction must also be made accessible.

The law does not clearly define what many of its terms mean, and does not even explain exactly who will qualify as *handicapped*. Some claim that up to forty percent of America's labor force may qualify as handicapped. The law includes people with emotional illnesses, AIDS, dyslexia, and past alcohol or drug addictions; as well as hearing, sight, and mobility impairments. Of course, this law will provide lots of work for lawyers who will sue landlords and businesses.

What is *reasonable* will usually depend upon the size of the business. Small businesses will not have to make major alterations to their premises if the expense would be an undue hardship. Even large businesses would not have to have shelving low enough for people in wheelchairs to reach as long as there was an employee to assist the person. In addition, there are tax credits for businesses of less than thirty employees and less than one million dollars in sales. For more information on these credits, obtain IRS forms 8826 and 3800 and their instructions.

Some of the changes that must be made to property to make it more accessible to the disabled are:

- Installing ramps
- Widening doorways
- Making curb cuts in sidewalks
- Repositioning shelves
- Repositioning telephones
- Removing high pile, low density carpeting
- Installing a full-length bathroom mirror

Both the landlord and the tenant can be liable if the changes are not made to the premises. Most likely, the landlord would be liable for common areas and the tenant for the areas under his or her control. However, since previous leases did not address this new statute, either party could conceivably be held liable.

PENALTY. Injunctions and fines of $50,000 for the first offense or $100,000 for subsequent offenses.

EXEMPTIONS. Private clubs and religious organizations are exempt from this law.

North Carolina Discrimination Law

The North Carolina Fair Housing Act (N.C.G.S. Chapter 41A) makes it unlawful for any person engaging in the leasing or rental of real property to discriminate against someone on the basis of race, religion, sex, national origin, handicapping condition, or familial status. Laws regarding familial status protects tenants with children. The state statute mirrors the federal Fair Housing Act. The reason for a duplicate state statute is to give victims of discrimination a state remedy that may be easier to pursue than the federal one. The statute does not require apartment owners to make all areas accessible to the handicapped.

Local Laws

Landlords should check their city and county ordinances before adopting a discriminatory policy such as an "adult only" complex.

Court Cases

The following court cases can give some guidance as to what types of actions are outlawed.

- It is sex discrimination to not include child support and alimony in an applicant's income. *U.S. v. Reese*, 457 F.Supp. 43 (D. Mont. 1978).
- It is not illegal to require a single parent and a child of the opposite sex to rent a two-bedroom rather than a one-bedroom apartment. *Braunstein v. Dwelling Managers, Inc.*, 476 F.Supp. 1323 (S.D.N.Y. 1979).
- It was found not to be illegal to limit the number of children allowed. *Fred v. Koknokos*, 347 F.Supp. 942 (E.D.N.Y. 1972). (But there may be a different interpretation under the 1988 amendment. Also, be sure to check local ordinances.)
- It is illegal to segregate the people in an apartment complex. *Blackshear Residents Organization v. Housing Authority of the City of Austin*, 347 F.Supp. 1138 (W.D.Tex. 1972).
- A company that used only caucasian models in its housing ads was ordered to pay $30,000 in damages. (The judge overruled the jury's recommended $262,000!) *Ragin v. Macklowe*, No. 88 Civ. 5665(RWS), U.S. D.C. S.D.N.Y., Aug. 25, 1992.

Agreements to Lease

What are your rights if a tenant agrees to rent your unit but then backs out? An agreement to enter into a lease may be a valid and binding contract even if a lease has not yet been signed.

> ***Note:*** An agreement to lease is enforceable if it is clear, definite, and complete. Even where there are no witnesses, a series of letters between the parties may be enough evidence of an agreement to enter into a lease. Remember, your actions can be as important as the words written in a document.

As a practical matter, it will probably not be worth the time and expense to sue someone for breaching an oral agreement to lease. Whether a landlord could keep a deposit after a prospective tenant changed his or her mind would depend upon the facts of the case and the understanding between parties. Writing "non-refundable" on the deposit receipt would work in the landlord's favor.

Leases and Rental Agreements

There are different opinions as to whether a landlord should use a lease with a set term (such as one year), or an open-ended agreement. Some argue that they would rather not have a lease so they can get rid of a tenant at any time. The disadvantage is that the tenant can also leave at any time, which means the unit may be vacant during the slow season.

Rental Agreements

In all cases, even month-to-month or week-to-week tenancies, there should be a written agreement between the parties. If the landlord does not want to tie up the property for a long period of time, he or she can use a Rental Agreement which states that the tenancy is month-to-month or week-to-week, but which also includes rules and regulations which protect the landlord. (See form 6.)

LEASES

A lease is a rental agreement which is for a set term. It can be as short as a few weeks or for several years.

REQUIRED CLAUSES

The minimum elements which a lease must contain to be valid are:

- Name of lessor (landlord) or agent
- Name of lessee (tenant)
- Description of the premises
- Rental rate
- Starting date
- Granting clause ("Lessor hereby leases to Lessee...")

(Actually, there have been cases where a lease has been held to be valid where one or more of these terms has been omitted if there was an objective means to determine the missing term; but such exceptions are beyond the scope of this book.)

MANAGEMENT DISCLOSURE

At or before the beginning of a residential rental, the landlord should disclose to the tenant either his name and address or the name and address of his agent. Generally, the agent, if any, retains authority until the tenant is given written notice of a change of agent. In most cases, the landlord's name and address in the lease or rental agreement is sufficient and no other notice need be given. If an agent collects rent after he is discharged and absconds with the money, it is the landlord's loss if he did not inform the tenants in writing that the agent no longer had authority to collect rents.

LEAD PAINT DISCLOSURE

In 1996, the Environmental Protection Agency and the Department of Housing and Urban Development issued regulations requiring notices to be given to tenants of rental housing built before 1978 that there may be lead-based paint present and that it could pose a health hazard to children. This applies to all housing except housing for the elderly or zero-bedroom units (efficiencies, studio apartments, etc.) It also requires that a pamphlet about lead-based paint, titled *Protect Your Family From Lead in Your Home,* be given to prospective tenants. The recommended disclosure form is included in this book as form 29.

The rule is contained in the *Federal Register*, Vol. 61, No. 45, March 6, 1996, pages 9064-9088. More information, and copies of the pamphlet, can be obtained from the National Lead Information Clearinghouse at 1-800-424-5323. The information can also be obtained at the following website: http://www.nsc.org/nsc/ehc/ehc.html

SUGGESTED CLAUSES

The following types of provisions are not required by any law, but are suggested by the author to avoid potential problems during the tenancy.

- Security and/or damage deposit
- Last month's rent
- Use clause (limiting use of the property)
- Maintenance clause (spelling out who is responsible for which maintenance)
- Limitation on landlord's liability
- Limitation on assignment of the lease by tenant
- Clause granting attorney's fees for enforcement of the lease
- Clause putting duty on tenant for own insurance
- Late fee and fee for bounced checks
- Limitation on number of persons living in the unit
- In a condominium, a clause stating that tenant must comply with all rules and regulations of the condominium
- Requirement that if locks are changed landlord is given a key (forbidding tenants to change locks may subject the landlord to liability for a break-in)
- Limitation on pets
- Limitation on where cars may be parked (not on the lawn, etc)
- Limitation on storage of boats, etc. on the property
- In a single family home or duplex a landlord should put most of the duties for repair on the tenant

- In commercial leases there should be clauses regarding the fixtures, insurance, signs, renewal, eminent domain, and other factors related to the business use of the premises
- To protect the landlord if it is necessary to dispose of property left behind by a tenant a clause outlining what the landlord plans to do with the property should be in the lease (see "Abandoned Property by Tenant" in chapter 8)

For an explanation and analysis of each of the different clauses used in residential and commercial leases and suggestions on how to negotiate, see *How to Negotiate Real Estate Leases*, by Mark Warda, available through your local bookstore, or directly from Sphinx Publishing by calling 1-800-226-5291.

ORAL LEASES

A lease of property for less than one year does not have to be in writing to be valid. Oral leases have been held up in court. If there is a disagreement over the existence or terms of an oral lease, it just depends upon who sounds more believable to the judge.

How will the Court determine who is telling the truth? The magistrate or judge will consider several factors including the following:

- Which party appears to be telling the truth based on their ability to recall and recite their version of the events
- Which party's version of the events is more consistent with the uncontroverted facts
- Which party's version of the events is more likely to have occurred

Courts are also more likely to believe the party who is the most articulate, calm, and polite in their demeanor.

PROBLEM CLAUSES

UNCONSCIONABLE

If a judge feels that a rental agreement is grossly unfair she may rule that it is *unconscionable* and unenforceable. In such a case, she may ignore the entire lease or may enforce only parts of it. Therefore, making your lease too strong may defeat your purpose. There is not much guidance as to what may or may not be unconscionable so the judge may use her discretion.

Waivers of Liability or Rights

If either of the following clauses are included in a lease, the clause is void and unenforceable; and a tenant suffering damages because of the clause may recover money from the landlord for any losses so caused.

- ☛ A clause waiving the rights, remedies, or requirements of the North Carolina Landlord/Tenant Law
- ☛ A clause limiting the liability of the landlord to the tenant or of the tenant to the landlord

Waivers in Commercial Leases

In a commercial lease, a tenant may waive rights which may not be waived in a residential lease. A commercial lease spells out nearly all of the rights and obligations of the parties. The statutes concerning landlord/tenant law are very limited in scope, so it is important to spell everything out carefully in the lease.

Hidden Clauses

If a lease contains a clause which might be considered controversial, it should not be buried in the lease. It should be pointed out to, and initialed by, the tenant. For example, a clause relieving a landlord of liability for damage to a tenant's property may be ignored if the landlord doesn't specifically point it out to the tenant.

Limiting Similar Businesses

Provisions in a lease which limit the landlord's right to lease other space to similar businesses should be strictly construed. For example, where a lease provided that a lessee would be the only "appliance store" in a shopping center, it was legal for the landlord to lease to a department store which also sold ranges, refrigerators, freezers, etc.

Options

Options to Renew

Both residential and nonresidential leases may contain clauses which grant the tenant an option to extend the lease for another term or several terms. Often these options provide for an increase in rent during the renewal periods.

Here are three key points to consider with respect to options to renew:

- An option to renew a lease is valid and enforceable, even if not all of the terms are outlined
- Some terms may be left open for future negotiation or arbitration, but where no terms are stated the court can assume that the terms will be at the same terms as the original lease
- Leases which can be renewed indefinitely are not favored by the court and where doubt exists as to the terms they may be limited to one renewal term

Options to Purchase

If a lease contains an option to purchase, it will usually be enforceable exactly according to its terms.

Where a tenant continued renting the property as a tenant at will after his lease expired, the court ruled his option to purchase the property expired at the end of the lease.

Forms

The landlord should be careful to choose a good lease form. Some forms on the market do not comply with North Carolina law and can be dangerous to use.

Forms in This Book

Forms 4, 5, and 6 in this book are leases developed and used by the author. They are free of legalese and intended to be easily understandable by both parties. You may also need to use forms 29 and 30 as explained elsewhere in the text.

Signatures

If you do not have the proper signatures on the lease, you could have problems enforcing it or evicting the tenants.

Landlord If the property is owned by more than one person, it is best to have all owners sign the lease.

Tenant In most cases, it is best to have all adult occupants sign the lease so that more people will be liable for the rent. But in inexpensive rentals where evictions are frequent, having just one person sign will save a few dollars in fees for service of process.

Initials Some landlords have places on the lease for the tenant to place their initials. This is usually done next to clauses which are unusual or very strongly pro-landlord. This might be helpful because in one case a judge refused to enforce a clause which was "buried" on page two of the lease, even though the judge admitted it was highlighted! However, even initials might not help if a judge really doesn't like a clause.

Witnesses No witnesses are required for a lease of one year or less. A lease of over one year is not valid without two witnesses to the Landlord's signature.

Notary A lease does not need to be notarized to be valid. A landlord should not allow his signature on a lease to be notarized because the lease could then be recorded in the public records which would be a cloud on his title and could cause a problem when the property is sold.

Backing Out of a Lease

Rescission Contrary to the beliefs of some tenants, there is no law allowing a rescission period for a lease. Once a lease has been signed by both parties it is legally binding on them.

Fraud If one party fraudulently misrepresents a material fact concerning the lease, then the lease may be unenforceable.

IMPOSSIBILITY

If the lease states that the premises are rented for a certain purpose and it is impossible to use the premises for that purpose, the lease may not be enforceable.

Consider these two examples: Tommy Tenant rented property from Larry Landlord for the express purpose of operating a moving and storage business. However, the zoning laws made it illegal to operate the business on the premises. In this situation, the lease is not likely to be enforceable. However, if Tommy Tenant had rented the property for a moving and storage business but was unable to secure the necessary financing or insurance to open the business, the landlord will be successful in enforcing the lease.

ILLEGALITY

If a lease is entered into for an illegal purpose, it is void and unenforceable by either party.

N.C.G.S., Chapter 42, Article 7 permits expedited evictions of drug traffickers and other criminals. The statute is directed at tenants who engage in drug related activity and "other criminal activity that threatens the health, safety, or right of peaceful enjoyment of the entire premises by other residents or employees of the landlord." The law allows the magistrate or judge to order "complete eviction" of everyone in the premises, or to "partially evict" only certain family members who are engaging in illegal activity.

3 Handling Security Deposits

This chapter applies only to residential tenancies. North Carolina does not have statutes governing nonresidential security deposits.

Amount

North Carolina has enacted laws establishing the maximum amount of security deposit a landlord may require:

Week-to-week tenancy	Two weeks rent
Month-to-month tenancy	One and a half months rent
Terms greater than month-to-month	Two months rent

There is no restriction against charging less than these amounts. The decision to require less than these amounts must be based on the practical consideration of what is the most you can get without scaring away desirable tenants.

Bank Account

All types of damage, rent, pet, and other tenant advance deposits must be kept in a separate account "for the benefit of the tenant" unless a surety bond is posted (N.C.G.S § 42-50). The separate tenant account may be interest bearing or non-interest bearing, and the landlord cannot pledge the money, use it in any way, or mix it with his own money.

The security deposits from the tenant may be held in a trust account outside the State of North Carolina only if the landlord provides the tenant with an adequate bond in the amount of the deposits.

The above provisions will probably be a surprise to most landlords. Very few landlords or tenants are aware of these rules, and even fewer understand them. Because of the expenses of a surety bond, the small landlord is stuck with the separate account alternative. Where tenants come and go, and the deposit is several hundred dollars, banks would not be pleased with the opening and closing of accounts with each new tenant.

Technically, the landlord cannot commingle even $10 of his own in the account to keep it open. However, as a practical matter, a $5 or $10 deposit of a landlord's own money to keep an account open during periods when there were no security deposits on hand would probably not be considered an actionable violation of the statute. In fact, it appears that most small North Carolina landlords do not keep the funds separate and this is seldom brought up by tenants.

NOTICE

Under N.C.G.S. § 42-50, landlords or their agents must comply with the following rules:

☛ Within thirty days of receipt of a deposit, a written notice must be given in person or by mail to the tenant. Form 30 can be used for this purpose. The notice must include:

- The name of the bank or institution where the deposit is located
- The address of the bank or institution where the deposit is located
- The name of the insurance company providing the bond

- If any of the above information changes, a new notice must be given within thirty days

FORWARDING ADDRESS

If the tenant has not left a forwarding address, the notice must be sent to the property address even though you know the tenant is gone. (The tenant might have given a forwarding address to the post office.) If you would like to know the tenant's new address, you can write "ADDRESS CORRECTION REQUESTED" on the front of the envelope and the post office will send you the address for a small fee.

PERMITTED USES OF THE DEPOSIT

Landlords may apply a tenant's security deposit to the following:

- Tenants possible nonpayment of rent
- Damage to premises
- Nonfulfillment of rental period
- Unpaid bills which become a lien against the demised property due to the tenant's occupancy
- Costs of re-entering the premises after breach by the tenant
- Costs of removal and storage of tenant's property after a summary ejectment proceeding
- Court costs in connection with terminating a tenancy

LANDLORD'S OBLIGATION AT END OF RENTAL TERM

At the conclusion of the rental term, the money held as the security deposit must be applied for one of the purposes listed above, or it must be refunded to the tenant. In either situation, within thirty days after the end of the rental term and the tenant vacates the premises, the landlord must mail or deliver to the tenant a written itemization of the damage and any refund of the security deposit. The landlord can't retain an amount from the security which exceeds actual damages.

If the landlord does not have the tenant's address, the landlord may still apply the deposit to the damages after thirty days, but the landlord must hold the balance of the deposit for collection by the tenant for at least six months. There is no direction as to what to do with the deposit after six months. Most landlords keep the money.

OBJECTIONS TO DEDUCTIONS

If the tenant does not object to the deductions, the landlord has no problem. However, if the tenant objects, he or she may file a civil action in small claims court and ask the magistrate to order the landlord to return the balance or provide a detailed accounting of how the deposit was used. Landlords can survive a tenant's claim by maintaining good records, taking photographs of the damages, and keeping copies of receipts for repairs.

If the magistrate decides the landlord deliberately or willfully held a security deposit knowing he was not entitled to it, the magistrate can order the landlord to pay the deposit in addition to reasonable attorney fees.

WEAR AND TEAR

The landlord may deduct *damages* from a security deposit, but may not deduct normal wear and tear. What is normal wear and tear is a question of fact which only a judge or jury can decide, using a standard of reasonableness. A hole in a wall is clearly not normal. An apartment needing painting after a tenant lived there ten years is normal. Between these two obvious examples, you have to use your best judgment. If you have any doubts, you should get a second opinion from a disinterested person or an attorney. A landlord making a claim on a deposit should *always* take pictures of the damage.

If a security deposit claim goes to court, it is also good to have receipts for the repairs that were done. However, a court will probably allow a landlord to do the work himself and charge for the reasonable value of the work.

The following court cases involved damages:

- An Illinois court allowed a landlord to deduct $40 for cleaning a stove and refrigerator himself. *Evans v. International Village Apts.*, 520 N.E.2d 919 (Ill.App. 1988). Of course, it would be helpful to get a written estimate before doing the work yourself.
- A Florida court allowed a landlord to charge a tenant for the cost of a real estate agent's fee for finding a new tenant for a rental unit. *McLennan v. Rozniak*, 15 Fla.Supp.2d 42 (Palm Beach 1985).
- Some leases have clauses allowing a landlord to keep the entire deposit or a certain portion of it if the tenant leaves before the lease is up. Where the clause was considered a "liquidated damages" clause, it was usually upheld; but where it was considered a penalty, it was dismissed. It is not possible to say for certain whether a clause will be considered one or the other because judges have a wide leeway in their rulings. Usually, the decision depends upon who the judge considers the good guy and the bad guy in the case.
- In one case, an automatic $200 re-rental fee was considered acceptable. *Lesatz v. Standard Green Meadows*, 416 N.W.2d 334 (Mich.App. 1987).
- In another case, an automatic $60 cleaning fee was considered a penalty and therefore illegal. *Albregt v. Chen*, 477 N.E.2d 1150 (Ohio App. 1985).
- In a California case, an additional $65 fee in a lease resulted in a civil penalty against the landlord of $271,000 plus $40,000 in attorney fees. *People v. Parkmerced Co.*, 244 Cal.Rptr. 22 (Cal.App.Div. 1988).

Special Rules

Hotels and Motels

These security deposit rules do not apply to transient rentals by hotels and motels.

Public Housing These security deposit rules do not apply to instances in which the amount of rent or deposit, or both, is regulated by laws or rules of a public body, such as public housing authorities, or federal housing programs; including § 202, § 221(d)(3) and (4), § 236, or § 8 of the National Housing Act, other than for rent stabilization.

Renewals If a rental agreement is renewed, the security deposit is considered a new deposit. This means that when a lease is renewed, a new Notice of Holding Security Deposit (form 30), as explained on page 28, must be sent to the tenant.

Sale of the Property Upon sale of the property or a change of the rental agent, all deposits and interest must be transferred to the buyer or agent together with an accurate accounting.

4 Responsibility for Maintenance

Nonresidential Rentals

North Carolina statutes do not specify who is responsible for maintenance in nonresidential rentals. Therefore, all of the responsibilities should be spelled out in the lease.

Residential Apartments

The landlord's duties of maintenance are included in N.C.S.G. § 42-42. Under this law, the landlord must provide tenants with a "fit premises."

Unless the landlord and tenant agree that these shall be the tenant's responsibility, the landlord must make "reasonable provision" for:

- Exterminations of rats, mice, roaches, ants, wood-destroying organisms, and bedbugs
- Locks and keys
- Clean, safe condition of common areas
- Garbage removal and outside receptacles

These rules do not apply to mobile homes owned by tenants.

The landlord may require the tenant to pay for garbage removal, water, fuel, or utilities. The landlord is not responsible for conditions that are caused by the tenant, the tenant's family, or guests.

Landlord's have an obligation to comply with all applicable building and housing codes. They are "required to do whatever is necessary" to maintain the premises in a fit and habitable condition. At a minimum, landlords must ensure the premises are in "safe condition" for the tenant to reside. They must maintain in safe and operating order, and immediately repair, each of the following:

- Electrical
- Plumbing
- Sanitary
- Heating
- Ventilating
- Air Conditioning
- Any other facility or appliance required to be supplied by the building code

North Carolina law [N.C.G.S. § 42-42(a)(5)] also requires landlords to provide tenants with operable smoke detectors. Landlords have an obligation to replace and repair the smoke detector if the tenant notifies the landlord in writing that the detector is not operating. Unless the landlord and tenant agree to the contrary, the landlord must provide new batteries at the beginning of the lease term, but it is the tenant's responsibility to replace them during the tenancy. If the tenant fails to replace the batteries, the landlord will not be found to be negligent.

The landlord cannot evade his responsibilities because the tenant appears to have accepted his failure to comply with the North Carolina law [N.C.G.S. § 42-42(b)] to provide a habitable, safe, and fit premises; either before the lease was made, at the time it was made, or after it was made.

However, the law does not prohibit a landlord and tenant from entering into a written contract in which the tenant agrees to perform work or repairs on the premises. The contract must include adequate consideration (i.e., some form of payment or compensation other than staying on the premises) and must not be designed to allow the landlord to escape his or her obligations imposed by North Carolina law.

Code Violations

Landlords should be aware that governmental bodies can levy fines of hundreds of dollars a day for even minor violations. Ignoring notices of violation can be expensive.

Whenever you receive a governmental notice, you should read it very carefully and follow it to the letter. One landlord who sold his property and thought the problem was solved was fined $11,000 ($500 a day for the last twenty-two days he owned the property) for a violation. After you correct a violation, be sure that the governmental body which sent the notice gives you written confirmation that you are in compliance.

Warranty of Habitability

In recent years, the centuries-old theories of landlord/tenant law have been replaced with new obligations on landlords to protect their tenants. One of these is the "implied warranty of habitability" which has been accepted in over forty states. Under this doctrine, any time a dwelling unit is turned over to a tenant, the tenant is automatically given a warranty by the landlord that the premises are in a safe and habitable condition, and will remain so during the term of the lease.

Note: If a lease states that a tenant is responsible for maintenance, the landlord should not voluntarily do repairs. Otherwise, the landlord can be held to have taken over responsibility for the safety of the premises.

If something comes up that the tenant cannot handle, and the landlord would rather do it himself, he should have the tenant sign an agreement that the landlord will handle this one item, this one time, but that the landlord assumes no other responsibilities.

Tenant's Responsibilities

Under N.C.G.S. § 42-43, at all times the tenant must:

- Comply with all building, housing, and health codes
- Keep his part of the premises clean and sanitary
- Remove his garbage in a clean and sanitary manner
- Use and operate in a reasonable manner all electrical, plumbing, sanitary, heating, ventilating, air conditioning, and other facilities and appliances, including elevators
- Not destroy, deface, damage, impair, or remove any part of the premises or property belonging to the landlord; nor permit any person to do so
- Conduct himself, and require other persons on the premises with his consent to conduct themselves, in a manner that does not unreasonably disturb his neighbors or constitute a breach of the peace
- It is also the tenant's responsibility, unless there is an emergency, to notify the landlord in writing of needed repairs as soon as practicable

Landlord Liability 5

The law of liability for injuries and crime on rental property has changed considerably over the last couple decades. The law, which held for hundreds of years that landlords, were not liable was overturned and landlords are now often liable, even for conditions that are not their fault. This change was not made by elected legislators representing their constituents, but by appointed judges who felt tenants needed protection and landlords should give it to them.

Injuries on the Premises

Areas Under Landlord's Control

The landlord has a duty to inspect and repair common areas in a rental building with more than one unit. This rule does not apply to a single-family home, unless the parties have agreed that the landlord will assume this responsibility. In a duplex, a landlord may state in the lease that the tenants assume the duty to take care of the common areas.

If a tenant is injured in an area under the landlord's control, it does not necessarily mean that the landlord will be liable. Tenants have an obligation to notify the landlord of dangerous conditions and to exercise reasonable care and caution. If they fail to do so, the landlord will not be held liable.

AREAS NOT UNDER THE LANDLORD'S CONTROL

The general rule is that a landlord is not liable for injuries on parts of the premises that are not under his or her control, except in the following circumstances:

- Where there is a danger known to the landlord
- Where there is a violation of law in the condition of the premises
- Where there is a pre-existing defect in construction
- Where the landlord undertakes to repair the premises or is required by the lease to do the repairs
- Where the landlord did a negligent act
- Where the premises was a *nuisance* at the time of making the lease or would become one upon tenant's expected use of the premises

CASES HOLDING A LANDLORD NOT LIABLE

The following are cases which held that a landlord was ***not*** liable for injuries. It must be kept in mind that the holdings in some of the earlier cases may have been modified by the rulings in later cases.

- Where the daughter of a guest of a tenant ran through a sliding glass door, the landlord was not liable since he was not in possession of the premises. He had no duty to ascertain that the glass was not safety glass, and had no duty to put decals on the glass. *Fitzgerald v. Cestari*, SC, No. 75,538, Nov. 8, 1990.
- Where a tenant was bit by rats in an apartment, the landlord was not liable because the tenant could not show the landlord was negligent in not keeping his apartments substantially rodent-free. *Floyd v. Jarrell*, 197 S.E.2d 229 (1973).
- Where the landlord furnishes lights with switches which are operable and convenient, he is not expected to foresee that a tenant would fail to turn on the lights when using the stairs, or, where two stairways are available, that the tenant would choose to use the less safe stairway. *Harris v. Nachamsom Department Stores*, 100 S.E.2d 323 (1957).
- Where the child of the tenant was injured when another child threw a can containing a caustic substance in his face as he was

playing in the yard of the landlord's apartment building, the landlord was not liable for failing to make reasonable and proper inspection to discover and remove the dangerous substance. *Watt v. Housing Authority of Charlotte*, 141 S.E.2d 11 (1965).

- Where an action was brought against a building manager for injuries sustained to an infant who fell through a screened second story window, the court held that the housing code only required screens to keep out insects, and that the failure to install protective screens that would have prevented the fall was not negligence. *Mudusar v. V.G. Murray & Co.*, 100 N.C. App. 395, 396 S.E. 2d 325 (1990).
- Where the tenant never notified the landlord about a problem with the staircase and could not establish solid evidence that the landlord actually knew of the dangerous condition, the court stated that the tenant's knowledge of problems with the staircase placed the burden on the tenant to either correct the problem or notify the landlord of the need for repairs. *Diorio v. Penny*, 331 N.C. 726, 417 S.E.2d 457 (1992).
- Where wooden beams in an old chimney ignited, and the rented dwelling was destroyed by fire, the landlord was not liable because the existence of the beams was not readily detectable by an inspection of the house. Also, there was no previous history of any problems with the chimney. *Bradley v. Wachovia Bank & Trust Co.*, N.A., 90 N.C. App. 581, 369 S.E.2d 86 (1988).

Cases Holding a Landlord Liable

The following cases are examples of when a landlord ***was*** held liable for injuries to a tenant or a guest:

- The landlord was liable where a hole caused by the removal of a bush was an unsafe condition on the landlord's premises. The landlord had notice of the unsafe condition but failed to repair it, and the landlord's failure to repair the condition caused the tenant's injury. *Baker v. Duhan*, 75 N.C. App 191, 330 S.E.2d 53 (1985).

- Where the rear steps of the apartment collapsed and injured the tenant, the landlord was liable because he was negligent in permitting the steps to remain defective when he knew, or should have known, the steps were in disrepair. *Brooks v. Francis,* 57 N.C. App. 556, 291 S.E.2d 889 (1982).
- Where the landlord allowed the natural accumulation of ice to remain on the common areas of the premises, the landlord was held liable for failing to clear an icy sidewalk on which the tenant fell and was injured. *Lenz v. Ridgewood Associates*, 55 N.C. App 115, 284 S.E.2d 702 (1981).

CONTRIBUTORY NEGLIGENCE

If it is found that the tenant was also negligent and their own conduct contributed to their injury, the landlord may be released of liability or the landlord's liability may be lessened.

LANDLORD'S WARRANTY OF HABITABILITY

The North Carolina legislature reversed centuries of landlord/tenant law by adopting the theory of the *landlord's warranty of habitability* for residential property. This was explained in more detail in chapter 4. The landlord warranty of habitability does not apply to nonresidential rentals.

PROTECTION FROM LIABILITY FOR INJURIES

The basis for liability in these cases is that the landlord breached a duty to keep the premises safe. If a landlord puts the duty to keep the premises safe on the tenant, there will be less likelihood that the landlord can be held liable. North Carolina law allows a landlord to put certain duties of maintenance on the tenant in a single-family dwelling or duplex. A non-residential lease can probably do the same. But in a multi-family building, the landlord cannot avoid the burden of making sure the premises are safe at all times.

Note: A landlord cannot immunize himself against liability for his own negligent actions. For example, the courts will not uphold a contract between a landlord and tenant which protects the landlord from liability in the event the landlord's negligence is the cause of a tenant's injury.

The result of all this is that the landlord is the insurer of the safety of tenants, and must, therefore, carry adequate insurance to cover any liability. Many landlords are raising rents to compensate for this additional insurance expense.

Crimes against Tenants

Another area where liability of landlords has been greatly expanded is in the area of crimes against tenants. The former theory of law was that a person cannot be held liable for deliberate acts of third parties. This had been the theory for hundreds of years, but has recently been abandoned in favor of a theory that a landlord must protect his tenants from crimes.

The theory has been stated to be that, where the landlord can foresee the possibility of criminal attack, the landlord must take precautions to prevent it. But some have said that this means any time an attack is possible, the landlord must protect the tenant. This would include nearly every tenancy, especially in urban areas. New Jersey has gone so far as to hold landlords strictly liable for every crime committed on their property, whether or not they knew there was a risk or took any precautions. This liability for crime, unlike the warranty of habitability, applies to both residential and commercial tenancies. However, it has not been extended to single family homes yet.

- 🕮 In a case in Florida, where owners of an apartment complex knew about the "sexually aberrant and bizarre behavior" of a tenant's child, they were liable when that child committed a sexual assault upon another child. In this case, the landlords wanted to evict the family, but the mother begged to stay and the landlords decided to be nice and let her stay a while longer. *Lambert v. Doe*, 453 So.2d 844 (Fla. 1 DCA 1984).

- In a case in Texas, a woman was awarded $17 million when she was raped by someone who broke into the management office and stole apartment keys. She had previously asked for a lock which could not be opened from the outside, but the management refused, saying they needed access to all units.

Protection from Liability for Crimes

The law is not clear in North Carolina as to just how far courts will go in holding landlords liable for crimes against tenants. A clause in a lease that makes a tenant responsible for locks and security may provide some protection to landlords in some situations, especially in single-family homes and duplexes.

But in some inner-city apartment complexes, where crime is common, landlords may be required to provide armed guards or face liability. Again, insurance is a must and this additional cost will have to be covered by rent increases. Isn't it interesting that homeowners cannot get insurance for crimes such as rape, but that tenants get free insurance out of the landlord's pocket?

Crimes by Tenants against Nontenants

In one case where a commercial tenant was selling counterfeit goods with such trademarks as Rolex and Polo, a United States District Court held that the landlords could be held liable if they knew of the activities of the tenants and did nothing to stop them. *Polo Ralph Lauren Corp. v. Chinatown Gift Shop*, 93 CIV 6783 TPG (United States District Court for the Southern District of New York, June 21, 1994).

6 Changing the Terms of the Tenancy

Assignment or Sublease by Tenant

As a general rule, unless it is prohibited in a lease, a landlord cannot stop a tenant from assigning his or her lease to someone else, or from subletting all or a portion of the premises.

ASSIGNMENT — An *assignment* is where a tenant assigns all of his or her interest in a lease to another party who takes over the tenant's position and deals directly with the landlord. The original tenant is called the *assignor* and the new tenant is the *assignee*.

SUBLEASE — A *sublease* is where the tenant enters into a new agreement with a third party who deals solely with the original tenant. The original tenant is called the *sublessor* and the new tenant is the *sublessee*.

VALIDITY — An assignment of lease for more than three years must be in writing in order to be enforceable in court. *Herring v. Volume Merchandise, Inc.*, 106 S.E.2d 197 (1958)

LIABILITY — If a lease contains an agreement to pay rent and the landlord does not release the tenant upon the assignment, the landlord may sue the original tenant if the new tenant defaults.

WAIVER — If a landlord knowingly accepts rent from an assignee or a sublessee of a lease, the landlord waives his right to object to the assignment. But if the landlord was unaware of the assignment, it does not constitute a waiver.

APPROVAL Some leases provide that a lease may only be assigned with the approval of the landlord. However, these clauses are not always enforced.

- A lease that does not allow subleases doesn't preclude assigning. Similarly, a lease that prohibits assigning doesn't preclude sublease. Specific language is important because these provisions will be strictly construed by the courts. *Rogers v. Hall*, 227 N.C. 363, 42 S.E.2d 347 (1947).
- Unless it is expressly defined in the lease agreement, there is no requirement that the landlord's withholding of consent to assignment or subleasing be reasonable. *Isbey v. Crews*, 55 N.C. App. 47, 284 S.E.2d 534 (1981).

SALE OF PROPERTY BY LANDLORD

A landlord has the right to sell property covered by a lease, but the new owner takes the property subject to the terms of the existing leases.

The new owner cannot cancel the old leases or raise the rent while the leases are still in effect (unless the leases have provisions allowing the landlord to do so). The following two general rules apply with respect to the sale of property by a landlord:

- The new owner must do any repairs to the property that the old owner would have had to do under the terms of the lease.
- In most cases, a landlord is relieved of his obligations under a lease upon sale of the property.

When selling property, a landlord must specify in the sales contract that the sale is subject to existing leases. Otherwise, the buyer may sue for failure to deliver the premises free and clear of other claims. At closing, the leases should be assigned to the buyer.

Raising the Rent

If a tenancy is for a set term (such as a one year lease) at a specified rent, the landlord cannot raise the rent until the term ends, unless such a right is spelled out in the lease. If the tenancy is month-to-month, the landlord would be able to raise the rent if he gives notice at least seven days prior to the end of the month. This is based upon the law that the landlord can cancel the tenancy by giving seven days notice. To raise the rent in a month-to-month tenancy, you can use form 9.

In such a case, the tenant would probably not have to give seven days notice if she decided not to stay at the end of the month. This is because, by raising the rent, the landlord would be terminating the previous tenancy and making the tenant an offer to enter into a new tenancy at a different rental rate.

Modifying the Lease

If you agree to modify the terms of your lease with a tenant, you should put it in writing. If you do not and you allow a tenant to do things forbidden in the lease, you may be found to have waived your rights. A simple modification form is included in this book as form 31.

7 Problems During the Tenancy

Landlord's Access to the Premises

Nonresidential

Under the historic principles of landlord/tenant law, which still apply to nonresidential tenancies, the landlord has no right to enter the premises unless it is given to the landlord in the lease.

Residential

Under North Carolina law, a landlord has no right to enter the premises unless this right is clearly stated in the lease agreement. The lease should be clear as to when and under what circumstances the landlord may enter. A landlord who unlawfully enters his or her tenant's residence may be sued by the tenant for trespass, or criminally prosecuted for breaking and entering.

A landlord may be justified to enter the leased premises in any of the following situations:

- With the consent of the tenant
- In case of emergency
- When the tenant unreasonably withholds consent
- If the tenant is absent from the premises for one-half of the rental period without notice

The landlord may enter the premises at any time if it is necessary to protect the premises. The landlord must not abuse the right of access or use it to harass the tenant. If you have trouble obtaining access to the premises, use form 8.

Violations by the Tenant

RENT DUE DATE

It is important that the lease agreement outlines exactly when the rent is due. If it fails to specify that the rent must be paid in advance, then, under common law, it will not be due until the end of the lease term. (This is because hundreds of years ago feudal tenants paid a share of their crops at the end of the season as rent.)

Note: If the lease is silent on when the rent is due, the parties actions will speak. For example, if Larry Landlord will not allow Thomas Tenant to move in until after paying the first week's rent, the courts will find that the parties have implicitly agreed that the rent is due in advance.

BAD CHECKS

North Carolina has a fairly effective bad check collection process. If you follow the rules, you will probably be able to collect on a bad check. Some counties have special divisions of the sheriff's department that actively help you collect on bad checks.

You must send the tenant a demand by certified mail, requiring that the tenant pay the amount of the check plus a processing fee which can not exceed $20.00. The demand must include the following:

- ☛ The check or draft number
- ☛ The reason the bank gave for returning the check
- ☛ A request that the person who wrote the check either correct the bank's error or satisfy the check within ten days

You can advise the tenant that legal action may be taken against him or her if payment is not made within a prescribed time period. However, it is illegal to make threats, harass, or deceive the person who wrote the bad check in order to get them to pay.

Damage to the Premises

If the tenant does intentional damage to the premises, the landlord can terminate the tenancy (see chapter 9) and can sue the tenant to recover the cost of repairs. This can be done by filing a complaint with a magistrate or in civil court.

Lease Violations

Before taking action to terminate a lease for a lease violation, the landlord must be certain that the lease is clear that a consequence of the violation is the termination of the lease. It is a mistake to assume that the lease can be terminated based on a lease violation because it contains provisions that require the timely payment of rent or that prohibit pets.

To clearly cover failure to pay rent, the following clause should be included in the lease agreement: "In the event the tenant fails to pay the rent as outlined in this lease agreement, the landlord may terminate this lease and assume possession of the premises."

To cover other types of violations, the following clause should be included in the lease agreement: "If the tenant fails to comply with any provision of this lease, the landlord reserves the right to terminate the lease and take legal action to regain possession of the property." It is not necessary to include this statement after every provision in the lease. The lease can include this statement once at the end of the lease.

> ***Note:*** The lease may allow the landlord to take immediate action to terminate the lease in the event of the breach, or it may require the landlord to give the tenant notice of the breach prior to taking any action.

Minor violations may be considered oversights, and the landlord may be wise to give the tenant an opportunity to *cure*, or correct, the violation; particularly if the tenant has a solid record of paying the rent in a timely manner. For example, if a good tenant buys a dog in violation of the lease, before initiating an eviction, give the tenant an opportunity to get rid of the dog.

Violations by the Landlord

Retaliatory Conduct

In 1979, the North Carolina legislature passed a law designed to protect a tenants right to seek "decent, safe and sanitary housing." Under N.C.G.S. § 42-37.1, it is unlawful for a landlord to evict a tenant for any of the following conduct which is done in good faith:

- Complaining or requesting the landlord or the landlord's agent to make repairs the landlord is obligated to make.
- Filing a complaint to a government agency about the landlord's violation of safety, health, or federal or state housing codes.
- Exercising their rights under state or federal law, or under the lease or rental agreement
- Creating or joining an organization promoting tenant's rights

Tenants who are facing a *summary ejectment action* (eviction) may raise *retaliatory eviction* as a defense to eviction if it can be shown that the tenant engaged in one of the protected acts listed above within twelve months of the landlord initiating the eviction action.

Landlords can still prevail in the eviction if they can show one of the following:

- The tenant failed to pay rent or breached another provision in the lease
- The tenant is holding over after the lease term has ended
- The tenant complaint is the result of the tenant's own negligence
- The landlord is unable to comply with the building code without removing tenant

Parties can not agree to waive the rights afforded to tenant's under this provision.

Sexual Harassment

It is a misdemeanor for a landlord, or their residential agent, to sexually harass any tenant or prospective tenant (N.C.G.S. § 395-1). A tenant might also be able to bring a civil action against a landlord who is guilty of sexual harassment. It is expensive for a landlord to defend himself against these types of lawsuits.

Landlords should adopt a sexual harassment policy and ensure that any agents are aware of the policy and following it. The following are examples of the type of conduct that should be avoided:

- Engaging in sexual relations with tenants or prospective tenants.
- Making sexually explicit comments to tenants or prospective tenants. You should also avoid making inappropriate comments in the presence of tenants.

Destruction of the Premises

If the property is damaged to the extent that it is no longer fit for the purpose it was leased without expending more than one year's rent, the damage was not the tenant's fault, and there is no provision in the lease dictating what should happen, the tenant may surrender premises in writing within ten days of the damage. The tenant will be required to pay a pro rata share of the rent when it becomes due. This will discharge the tenant from further rent payments.

8 Problems at the End of the Tenancy

Tenant Holding Over

Where the tenant holds over at the end of the lease term, the landlord must initiate a *summary ejectment action* to have the person removed from the premises.

Holding over, which is defined in N.C.G.S. § 42-26, refers to a tenant who continues to remain in the premises without the permission of the landlord after a demand is made for its surrender.

A tenant who is holding over may be dispossessed in these situations:

- The tenant holds over after his term has expired
- The tenant has done something or failed to do something that, according to the lease, would cause the lease to terminate

In a holding over case the landlord must establish both that:

1. The tenant was notified that the lease would end at the end of the term; and
2. At the end of the term, the tenant refused to vacate the premises.

Notice can be designated in the lease agreement. It can be oral, or written and issued by certified mail. The form the notice must take can also be agreed to in an oral agreement.

If there is no written agreement and the lease is for a definite period, no notice is required because the tenant knew lease would end at the end of the term.

The length of the lease term will determine the amount of notice that is required, as follows:

Year-to-Year	Month before end of term
Month-to-Month	A week before end of term
Week-to-Week	Two days before end of term

For a tenancy at will, which has no definite term, the landlord must give *reasonable* notice. What is reasonable will depend upon the circumstances; however, a landlord should allow the tenant sufficient time to vacate the premises. If the case goes to court, the magistrate will decide what is reasonable.

☛ In Section 8 Public Housing, and Section 236 Public Housing, a landlord cannot refuse to renew a lease without good cause.

Property Abandoned by Tenant

North Carolina law (N.C.G.S § 42-25.7) is clear that it is unlawful and against public policy for a landlord to take any action to discard, sell, or give away a tenant's personal property until they have successfully completed the summary ejectment action, the court granted them possession, and the sheriff has taken action to enforce the judgment.

What is Abandonment? A landlord can lawfully conclude that a tenant's personal property has been abandoned if it is clear that the tenant has voluntarily vacated the premises after the lease term has ended, and the landlord was not aware or notified of any extenuating circumstances which caused the premises to be vacated.

Abandonment Procedures There are basically four options available to landlords in dealing with a tenant's abandoned property:

1. Standard procedure
2. Removal by sheriff
3. Procedure if property valued at $500 or less
4. Procedure if property valued at less than $100

Each of these procedures is explained further below.

STANDARD PROCEDURE

Under N.C.G.S. § 42-25.9(g), ten days after obtaining lawful possession of the rental premises, the landlord can "throw away, dispose of, or sell" any personal property which has been abandoned by the tenant.

During the ten day period, the landlord may place the abandoned property in storage. If the tenant requests the property prior to the end of the ten day period, the landlord must return the property to the tenant.

If the landlord chooses to sell the property, he or she can do so at either a public or private sale. The landlord must send the tenant notice of the sale to their last known address seven days prior to the sale. The seven-day notice can run concurrently with the ten day notice. The written notice must include the following information:

- Date of sale
- Time of sale
- Place of sale

Proceeds (minus payment of unpaid rents, damages, storage fees, and costs associated with sale), upon request, must be returned to the tenant within ten days after the sale, or it should be returned to the county government where the rental property is located.

REMOVAL BY SHERIFF

Under N.C.G.S. § 42-36.2, the court can give the sheriff the authority to remove a tenant's personal property through the issuance of a writ or order. The sheriff must give the tenant notice of the approximate time they will be following through on the judge's order. The sheriff must remove the property at the time stated in the order unless:

- The landlord signs a written statement stating that the property can remain inside the premises. In these situations the sheriff can place a padlock on the premises. The cost of padlocking will be assessed to the tenant as part of the court cost.

- The landlord provides a written statement that the tenant has paid all outstanding obligations and the landlord no longer wishes to evict the tenant.

If the tenant does not take possession of their property, the sheriff can take the property to a storage company. The landlord must pay the cost of moving the property to storage and one month's storage.

If the sheriff makes this request and the landlord refuses to pay these costs, the sheriff will notify the court.

The landlord must assume responsibility for the property for ten days. During that time, they can't dispose of the property and must return it to the tenant if the tenant requests. After ten days the landlord is free to dispose of the property.

Property Valued at $500 or Less

Under N.C.G.S. § 42-25.9(d), if the personal property is valued at $500 or less, the landlord has the option to deliver the property to a non-profit organization, such as Goodwill or the Salvation Army, whose mission is to provide clothing or household goods to the indigent for free or at a discount price. The non-profit organization must agree to store the property separately for thirty days before selling or giving it away. They must also agree to return the property to the tenant if they claim it within that thirty-day period.

The landlord must post a notice on the rental property containing the name and address where the property is being held. The notice should not contain a description of the property being held. The landlord can choose to mail a copy of the notice to the tenant's last known address.

Property Valued at Less Than $100

Under N.C.G.S. § 42-25.9(h), if the personal property is valued at less than $100, the landlord can lawfully conclude the property is abandoned after five days and dispose of the property. The landlord must return the property to the tenant if they request it prior to the end of the five day period.

Terminating a Tenancy 9

A tenancy may be terminated in several ways. Unless the tenancy is terminated properly, the tenant may not be evicted. If you file an eviction without properly terminating the tenancy, the tenant may win the case and you may be ordered to pay damages to the tenant as well as the tenant's attorney fees.

Tenancies with No Specific Term

Even where there is no lease between the parties the law is strict about how the tenancy may be terminated. Any variation from these procedures can delay the eviction for months. But if done right, a tenant can be removed quickly.

RESIDENTIAL

Under N.C.G.S. § 42-14, if a residential unit is rented without a specific term, either party may terminate the rental by giving written notice as follows:

- Where the rent is paid yearly, the notice must be given at least one month prior to the end of the year.
- Where the rent is paid monthly, the notice must be given at least seven days prior to the end of the month.

- Where the rent is paid weekly, the notice must be given at least two days prior to the end of the week.

For example, if a tenant who pays rent monthly does not give notice at least seven days prior to the end of the month that they plan to terminate, the tenant is liable for rent for an additional month. Likewise, if a landlord wants to terminate a monthly rental, he or she must give the tenant notice at least seven days prior to the end of the month or the tenant may stay another month.

A tenancy may not be terminated in the middle of a term. For example, if a landlord or tenant on a monthly basis gives notice on August 12th that they wish to terminate the tenancy, then they may terminate effective August 31st (not August 19th). If they give notice on August 27th, then they may terminate the tenancy effective September 30th and not sooner. (Unless both parties agree.)

Expiration of Rental Term

When the term of a lease ends, the tenant is expected to vacate the property without notice. This is different from some states where a lease is presumed to be renewed unless the tenant gives the landlord notice that he or she is leaving. If you believe that a tenant may not be expecting to leave at the end of the lease, then you can use form 19.

Employment Rentals

The situation where a residential unit is provided without rent as part of employment is usually not covered by the landlord/tenant statutes. Therefore, the general rules regarding the formation, breach, and enforcement of contracts would apply. It would probably be prudent to consult an attorney about having an employee removed.

Military Rentals

North Carolina law (N.C.G.S. § 42-52) has special provisions for members of the United States Armed Forces who are either:

1. Officially transferred to a location that is fifty miles or more away from the leased premises
2. Discharged from active duty

In such circumstances, the tenant may terminate the tenancy by giving the landlord written notice and attaching a copy of the military orders or a verified statement from his or her commanding officer. The tenancy terminates thirty days after the landlord receives the notice.

Once the tenancy is terminated, the tenant must pay the rent prorated to the effective new date of termination. The rent will be due on the same date upon which the parties had previously agreed.

If the tenant has completed less than six months of the lease term, the landlord may recover any actual damages incurred due to the early termination of the lease, limited based upon how much of the lease term has been completed as follows:

- Less than six months of the lease term: One month's rent
- At least six months, but not more than nine months of the lease term: 1.5 month's rent

Early Termination by Tenant

Note on commercial tenancies: The early termination of a commercial (also called a non-residential) tenancy is governed by the terms of the lease. Therefore, the remainder of this section deals only with the termination of residential tenancies.

Destruction of the Premises If the premises are damaged or destroyed, other than by wrongful or negligent acts of the tenant, and if the premises "cannot be made reasonably fit," the tenant may immediately vacate the premises and terminate the rental after giving the landlord ten days notice. (For more information see "Destruction of the Premises" on page 51.)

Wrongful Surrender It is a misdemeanor for a tenant to "willfully, wrongfully and with the intent to defraud" surrender or turn over the tenancy unit to anyone other than the landlord or their agent.

Landlord's Noncompliance If the landlord materially fails to comply with his or her maintenance obligations or with the terms of the lease and does not comply after notice is given by the tenant, the tenant may terminate the rental and vacate the premises. However, the tenant must go to court in order to do so. Tenants cannot simply withhold rent.

Efforts to Cure If the landlord makes every reasonable effort to comply with his or her maintenance obligations and the noncompliance is beyond the control of the landlord, the parties may terminate or amend the rental agreement as follows:

- If the premises are not livable, the tenant may vacate and not be liable for rent as long as it remains unlivable
- If the premises are livable, the tenant may pay reduced rent based on the lost value of the premises

Remedies for Breach If the tenant breaches the lease by vacating early, the landlord has three options:

1. Retake the premises for the landlord's own account, thereby terminating all further liability of the tenant.
2. Retake the premises for the account of the tenant, re-let the premises, and hold the tenant liable for any difference in the rent received.
3. Do nothing, and sue the tenant for the lost rent as it comes due.

If the landlord opts to find a new tenant, he or she must make a good faith effort to do so and use the same efforts used previously or for other units. If the landlord has other vacant units, he or she does not have to rent out the tenant's unit first.

Early Termination by Landlord

Note on commercial tenancies: The early termination of a commercial (also called a non-residential) tenancy is governed by the terms of the lease. Therefore, the remainder of this section deals only with the termination of residential tenancies.

Grounds for Termination

A landlord may terminate a tenancy before the end of the term for three reasons: nonpayment of rent, breach of the lease other than nonpayment of rent, or the tenant engaging in criminal conduct.

Demand

North Carolina law (N.C.G.S § 42-3) requires landlord's to send tenants a written demand for any unpaid rent at least ten days prior to the landlord filing a court action to have the tenant removed. The law provides no guidelines as to the language or format of the demand, however, the demand should include a clear statement that it is a demand for past due rent.

Unless otherwise provided in the lease, there is no requirement that the landlord make a demand or send a notice prior to filing the court action in situations where the landlord wants to end the lease for reasons other than failure to pay rent.

It may be a good idea to send such a notice if the landlord wants to give an otherwise good tenant an opportunity to cure the problem; or if the landlord wants to give the tenant an opportunity to vacate the premises without having to file court action.

Delivery of the Demand

The demand may be mailed, hand-delivered, or posted on the tenant's door. If mailed, the tenant will probably be entitled to five extra days to allow for mailing time. The notice should only be posted if the tenant is absent from the premises.

PAYMENT OF RENT

Once the landlord accepts rent or the tenant pays rent after a known violation, the landlord can't terminate the rental for the period, but they may terminate it the next time rent comes due if the violation continues.

NONPAYMENT OF RENT DEMAND

If the tenant fails to pay the rent, the landlord may send the following ten day demand (see form 15):

> YOU ARE HEREBY NOTIFIED THAT YOU ARE INDEBTED TO ME IN THE SUM OF $________ FOR THE RENT AND USE OF THE PREMISES _*(address of premises, including county)*, NORTH CAROLINA, NOW OCCUPIED BY YOU AND THAT I DEMAND PAYMENT OF THE RENT OR POSSESSION OF THE PREMISES WITHIN THREE DAYS (EXCLUDING SATURDAY, SUNDAY AND LEGAL HOLIDAYS) FROM THE DATE OF DELIVERY OF THIS NOTICE, TO WIT: ON OR BEFORE THE _____ DAY OF _____________, _____. _*(Landlord's name, address and phone number)*___.

COMMON MISTAKES

The following are two of the more common mistakes landlords make, which can pose problems for obtaining an eviction:

Miscalculation of Ten Days. The most common reason for a landlord to lose an eviction is because he or she wrongly executed the ten-day demand. The most common mistake is getting the ten-day period wrong. If you make such a mistake, you can lose the case and be forced to pay the tenant's attorney fees. Two big problems have been that landlords do not know about North Carolina holidays and fail to calculate weekends. It should be noted that when a holiday falls on Sunday, Monday is considered a holiday; and that some counties have their own legal holidays. Also, judges may declare Rosh Hashanah, Yom Kippur, and Good Friday as court holidays. A full list of North Carolina legal holidays is included in appendix B in the back of this book. *Call your court clerk to see what days are "court observed holidays" in your area before preparing your ten day notice.* The law requires landlords to give at least ten days notice, however, in order to avoid a problem, it may be prudent to wait a few additional days before filing a legal action.

Mistatement of Amount Due. Another common mistake landlords make is in the amount of rent due. The notice should only include amounts due for rent, not late charges or utility bills. If the lease clearly states that late charges are part of the "rent," you ***may*** get away with including them; but at least one court has held that, even if these extras are included in the rent, they may not be included in the notice. If the ten day notice does include other charges, you may lose your case and be required to pay the tenant's attorney fees.

PAYMENT OF RENT

If a tenant attempts to pay the rent before the entry of the magistrate's judgment, the landlord must accept it (N.C.G.S. § 42-33). If the landlord wants to evict the tenant anyway, the only way to do it is if the tenant violates another clause in the lease. If the tenant attempts to pay the rent but the landlord refuses, and the tenant tenders the rent again in court, the magistrate will order the landlord to accept the rent and will dismiss the case. If the landlord accepts rent with the knowledge that the tenant is not complying with some other aspect of the lease, the landlord does not waive the right to evict for that noncompliance.

BREACH OF LEASE

As explained in chapter 7, before taking any action to terminate a tenancy, the landlord must be sure that the lease is clear that the consequence of a breach is the termination of the lease. Moreover, if the breach is curable, the landlord should use the notice referred to in chapter 7 to give the tenant an opportunity to cure the breach. As a general rule, the landlord should always assume a breach is curable unless it is really bad, such as intentional damage of property or continued unreasonable disturbance.

If the tenant repeats a noncompliance after receiving the notice, the landlord may terminate the tenancy by sending the following notice to the tenant (see form 16):

> YOU ARE ADVISED THAT YOUR LEASE IS TERMINATED EFFECTIVE IMMEDIATELY. YOU SHALL HAVE ____ DAYS FROM THE DELIVERY OF THIS LETTER TO VACATE THE PREMISES. THIS ACTION IS TAKEN BECAUSE ____
> ____.

You will need to fill in the number of days the tenant has to vacate (what is stated in the lease; or, if a period is not not stated in the lease, the amount of time you have determined to be reasonable.

Special Rules for Public Housing

For non-payment of rent in a public housing unit, the landlord must give the tenant fourteen days notice rather than a three day notice; and it must be mailed or hand delivered, not posted [24 CFR 866.4(1)(2)]. The notice must inform the tenant of his or her right to a grievance procedure. At least one court has held that both a fourteen-day notice and a three-day notice must be given. *Stanton v. Housing Authority of Pittsburgh*, 469 F.Supp. 1013 (W.D. Pa. 1977). But other courts have disagreed. *Ferguson v. Housing Authority of Middleboro*, 499 F.Supp. 334 (E.D. Ky. 1980).

- 🕮 The public housing authority must prove both that the tenant did not pay the rent, and that the tenant was at fault for not paying it. *Maxton Housing Authority v. McLean*, 328 S.E.2d (N.C. 1985).
- 🕮 A Louisiana court held that a tenant was not at fault because her former husband did not pay the child support. *Housing Authority of City of New Iberia v. Austin*, 478 So.2d 1012 (La.App. 1986) writ denied, 481 So.2d 1334 (La. 1986). (Did they think that it was the landlord's fault?)
- 🕮 One Florida court held that posting both a fourteen day notice and the state law required three day notice is too confusing. It suggested that the landlord only use a fourteen day notice or else deliver the three day notice so that the deadline was the same as for the fourteen day notice. *Broward Co. Housing Authority v. Simmons*, 4 F.L.W.Supp. 494 (Co.Ct. Broward 1996).

For breach of the terms of the lease other than payment of rent, a thirty-day notice must be given, except in emergencies, and it must inform the tenant of the reasons for termination, his or her right to reply, and his or her right to a grievance procedure [24 CPR 366(4)(1)]. If the tenant requests a grievance hearing, a second notice must be given, even if the tenant loses in the hearing. *Ferguson v. Housing Authority of Middleboro*, 499 F.Supp. 432 (E.D. Ky. 1980).

For nonpayment of rent, tenants must be given the three-day notice and be advised that, if there is a judicial proceeding, they can present a valid defense, if any. Service must be by first class mail, and hand delivered or placed under the door [24 CFR 450.4(a)].

For breach of the terms of the lease other than payment of rent, the tenant must first have been given notice that in the future such conduct would be grounds for terminating the lease. The notice of termination must state when the tenancy will be terminated, specifically why it is being terminated, and it must advise the tenant of the right to present a defense in the eviction suit (24 CFR 450).

The section of the law stating that acceptance or payment of rent is a waiver of any past noncompliance, does not apply to the portion of the rent that is subsidized. However, waiver will occur if legal action is not taken within forty-five days.

Under 24 CFR 882.215(c)(4), the landlord must notify the housing authority in writing at the commencement of the eviction proceedings. Also, the previous paragraph applies to section 8 housing as well.

Death of a Tenant

If a lease contains a clause binding the "heirs, successors, and assigns" of the lessee, the lease continues after the death of the tenant; unless cancelled by agreement of the lessor and the heirs. Otherwise, a lease is a personal contract which expires at death.

Options to Cancel

Generally, when a lease allows one party to cancel it at will, the lease is not considered binding and the courts will allow either party to cancel it at will. A lease will probably be held to be valid if the option to cancel is contingent upon some event.

Evicting a Tenant 10

Self-Help by Landlord

The only way a landlord may recover possession of a dwelling unit is if the tenant voluntarily surrenders it to the landlord or abandons it, or if the landlord gets a court order giving the landlord possession. As explained in more detail below, self-help methods such as shutting off electricity or changing locks can result in thousands of dollars in fines. Fortunately, the eviction process usually works quite quickly in North Carolina. In some cases, tenants' lawyers have abused the system and allowed non-paying tenants to remain in possession for months, but most of the time the system allows delinquent tenants to be removed quickly.

Retaliatory Conduct

Residential landlords are specifically forbidden to use self-help methods to evict tenants, even if the lease allows it. If a landlord directly or indirectly terminates utilities such as water, electricity, gas, elevators, lights, garbage collection, or refrigeration; or if the landlord locks up the unit or takes off the doors, windows, roofs, walls, etc., the landlord can be liable for damages of at least three times the tenant's actual damages, plus court costs and attorney's fees.

- 🕮 In a Missouri case, a landlord took the refrigerator, washing machine, and stove because the tenant failed to pay rent, and the tenant was awarded $10,000.00 in damages. *Smiley v. Cardin*, 655 S.W.2d 114 (Mo.Ct.App. 1983).

- In a District of Columbia case where purchasers of a tax deed to property kept changing the locks on the property, nailing the door shut, and nailing "for sale" signs on the property when the occupant was away, a jury awarded the occupant $250,000.00 in punitive damages. The purchasers had used those tactics to try to force the occupant to sue them, so that the government would have to defend the tax deed. The appeals court upheld the verdict. *Robinson v. Sarisky*, 535 A.2d 901 (D.C.App. 1988).
- In a Florida case, a landlord posted a three-day notice and when the tenant was absent from the premises he entered and removed her possessions. She testified in a lawsuit that her possessions were all heirlooms and antiques and since the landlord had disposed of them, he could not prove otherwise. She was awarded $31,000.00 in damages. *Reynolds v. Towne Mgt. of Fla., Inc.*, 426 So.2d 1011 (Fla. 2 DCA 1983).

Surrender or Abandonment

To surrender a dwelling, a tenant must tell the landlord that he or she is leaving or leave the keys. It can be presumed that a tenant abandoned a dwelling if the tenant has been absent for half of the rental term (unless the rent is current or notice is given). In some cases, such as where all of a tenant's possessions are gone and the electricity has been turned off at the tenant's request, a landlord may be safe in assuming abandonment; but if the matter went to court, the landlord could lose.

Settling with the Tenant

Although in ninety percent of all North Carolina evictions, the tenants do not answer the complaint and the landlord wins quickly; some tenants can create nightmares for landlords. Clever tenants and legal aid lawyers can delay the case for months, and vindictive tenants can destroy the property with little worry of ever having to pay for it. Therefore, in some cases, lawyers advise their clients to offer the tenant a cash settlement to leave. For example, a tenant may be offered $200 to be out of the premises and leave it clean within a week. Of course it hurts to give money to a tenant who already owes you money, but it could be cheaper than the court costs, vacancy time, and damages to the premises. Then again, an old American saying is, "Millions for defense but not one cent for tribute." You'll have to make your own decision based upon your tenant.

Grounds for Eviction

A tenant can be evicted for violating one of the terms of the lease, for engaging in criminal conduct, or for failing to leave at the end of the lease. The most common violation is that the tenant has failed to pay the rent, but a tenant can also be evicted for violating other terms of the rental agreement, such as disturbing other tenants.

Terminating the Tenancy

It is an ancient rule of law that an eviction suit cannot be filed until the tenancy is legally terminated. There are cases from the 1500s in which evictions were dismissed because the landlord failed to properly terminate the tenancy. If you make the same mistake, don't expect the judge to overlook it. What the judges often do is order the landlord to pay the tenant's attorney fees.

Termination for Cause

The tenancy may terminate by natural expiration or by action by the landlord. If you need to evict a tenant whose tenancy has not expired, you should carefully read the previous chapter and follow the procedures to properly terminate the tenancy.

Termination by Expiration

If parties to a rental agreement do not agree to renew or extend the agreement, it automatically ends at its expiration date. (This is different from some other states where the lease is automatically renewed unless notice is given that it is not being renewed.)

Using an Attorney

The landlord/tenant statutes provide that the loser in a landlord/tenant case can be charged with the winner's attorney fees. Because of this, it is important to do an eviction carefully. In some cases, the tenant may just be waiting for the eviction notice before leaving the premises. In such a case, the landlord may regain the premises no matter what kind of papers he files. But in some cases, tenants with no money and no defenses have gotten free lawyers, paid for by our tax dollars, who find technical defects in the case. This can cause a delay in the eviction and cause the landlord to be ordered to pay the tenant's attorney fees. A simple error in a landlord's court papers can cost him the case.

A landlord facing an eviction should consider the costs and benefits of using an attorney compared to doing it without an attorney. One possibility is to file the case without an attorney and hope the tenant moves. If the tenant stays and fights the case, an attorney can be hired to finish the case. Some landlords who prefer to do their evictions themselves start by paying a lawyer for a half-hour or hour of time to review the facts of the case and point out problems. We know of some attorneys who loan this book to their clients and advise them as questions arise. Whenever a tenant has an attorney, the landlord should also have one.

> 🕮 A winning tenant was awarded $8,675.00 in attorney fees, which was figured at $150 an hour and then doubled.

It is, of course, important to find an attorney who knows landlord/tenant law and charges reasonable fees. There are many subtleties of the law that can be missed by someone without experience. Some attorneys who specialize in landlord/tenant work charge very modest fees, such as $75 or $100 to file the case; and the same amount for a short hearing, unless the case gets complicated. Others charge an hourly rate that can add up to thousands of dollars. You should check with other landlords or a local apartment association for names of good attorneys, or you might try calling the manager of a large apartment complex in the area.

If you get a security deposit at the beginning of the tenancy and start the eviction immediately upon a default, then the deposit should be nearly enough to cover the attorney's fee.

Who Can Sue?

An owner can represent himself in court and does not need an attorney. As a general rule, no one can represent another person in court except a licensed attorney and only an attorney can represent a corporation. Not even a corporate officer can represent a corporation, except in small claims court. It is a criminal offense for a non-lawyer to represent another party in court.

In many instances the landlord will hire a rental agent to manage the property. The rental agent will be responsible for dealing with the tenant—renting the property, signing leases, collecting rent payments, and handling complaints. The rental agent in these situations, where they have first-hand information regarding the facts supporting eviction, are permitted to sign the complaint and appear in court on behalf of the landlord. However, the landlord should be named as the plaintiff. If they are not, the action is subject to dismissal.

Court Procedures

An eviction is started by filing a *complaint* against the tenant in small claims court and paying the filing fee. The suit must be filed in small claims court and an extra copy of the complaint must be provided for each defendant you are suing. The copies are *served* upon the tenants by the sheriff or by a private process server. A process server may cost a few dollars more than the sheriff, but can often get service quicker and may be more likely to serve the papers personally which will allow you to get a money judgment.

Small claims court is not like civil district court. The procedures are different and the magistrates are accustomed to dealing with landlords who have no lawyer. Many landlords successfully handle their own cases, and we have included in this book an explanation of the process along with the necessary forms. To get a picture of the eviction process, see the eviction flowcharts in appendix B.

> ***Note:*** Occasionally, someone will write to us and say that they followed this book but the judge did not follow the rules or gave the tenants extra time to move. Remember, usually a case will go smoothly, but judges do make mistakes. If your case gets complicated, you should invest in an experienced landlord/tenant attorney who can finish your case quickly.

Complaint

To begin an eviction you must complete a complaint and file it with the clerk of court. The complaint must be filed in the county where at least one of the tenants is a resident. Many landlords make the mistake of filing summary ejectment actions in the county where the landlord lives or operates his or her business. The magistrate will have no choice but to dismiss the case if it is filed in the wrong place.

Landlords should ensure they are filing the action against the proper person. The name of any person who signed the rental agreement should be listed as a defendant on the complaint. If the defendant is a corporation, use the corporate name as defendant. If the defendant is a business which is not incorporated, the business owner's name should be used for the defendant.

North Carolina has published standard complaint forms for summary ejectment actions. These are printed in a carbonless copy format, so it will not be necessary to make copies if you obtain the forms from the court. Form 19 is a summary ejectment complaint. The form should cover the majority of claims associated with the eviction of a residential tenant. However, a more detailed complaint will be needed in non-residential or evictions, which are generally filed in District Court because the amount in dispute exceeds $3,000.00 (which is the jurisdictional limit that is imposed in small claims court).

It may be necessary to consult an attorney prior to filing a summary ejectment action in District or Superior Court. There are many technical rules about what must be included in the complaint.

> ***Note:*** The summary ejectment complaint (form 19) published by North Carolina does not need to be notarized. However, if you prepare your own complaint for a non-residential eviction, it will need to be notarized. Appendix C includes a Verification (form 21) which you should have notarized and attach to your complaint.

Seeking Damages. More information about obtaining a money judgment against the tenant is contained later in this chapter. However, you should read that section before filing your eviction, since some of the forms in the eviction will be different.

Public Housing. In Section 8 housing, under the Code of Federal Regulations § 882.215(c)(4), the local housing authority must be notified in writing before the tenant can be served with the eviction.

Service of Process

Once the complaint has been filed, the copies must be served on the tenants, along with a summons. A *summons* is a legal document that tells the tenant that he or she must reply to your complaint or have a judgment entered against him or her. In an eviction, a tenant has to respond prior to the date stated in the summons.

Service of process (the legal term for officially notifying a defendant) can be done by either the sheriff or a process server. In some areas where the sheriff will be unable to handle the service for several days, a private process server can offer the advantage of quick service. A process server can be found by checking with the clerk or looking in the phone book under *Process Servers* or *Detective Agencies*. The sheriff's fee for serving process is $20; private process servers will cost more.

North Carolina has a Magistrate Summons (form 22) which is used with the standard Summary Ejectment Complaint (form 19). The summons includes a space the clerk uses to schedule the hearing. When the tenant receives the summons, the information the clerk filled in on the summons will notify the tenant of the time, date, and place of the hearing. Therefore, the landlord will not have to complete any separate form to notify the tenant of the court date.

Service of process can also be completed by mailing a copy of the summons and complaint to the tenant by registered or certified mail, return receipt requested. If you choose this option, you must file a Affidavit of Service by Registered or Certified Mail (form 32) with the clerk and attach a copy of the return receipt from the post office. You can also bring this form to court on the day of the hearing.

Answer

After the papers have been served upon the tenants, they have until any time prior to the hearing (excluding Saturdays, Sundays, and legal holidays) in which to file an answer (or to vacate the premises). Most tenants leave at this point.

If the tenant fails to file an answer or appear in court, the landlord does not automatically win by default but must still appear in court and prove his or her case.

Hearing

If the tenant has a lawyer, you should also get one. A small mistake by you could cost you the case, and you may have to pay the tenant's attorney fees, which could amount to thousands of dollars. (We know, you are already losing enough money and you can't afford hundreds of dollars in attorney fees for this deadbeat tenant. But, an occasional bad tenant is a risk of investing in real property, and the cost should be factored into your return. Next time, screen your tenant better or get a bigger deposit.)

The landlord should come to court armed with the following documentation (bring an additional copy for the magistrate):

- Lease or rental agreement
- Ten Day Demand for Past Due Rent
- Affidavit of Service by Registered or Certified Mail
- Complaint and Summons
- Photographs of damages
- Receipts/estimates for repairs
- Any relevant correspondence between the landlord and tenant
- Affidavits from witnesses who can attest to the tenant's breach
- Any documentation that can help substantiate breach
- A copy of this book.

If the tenant shows up with an attorney and you were not told previously that an attorney was involved, you should ask the judge for a continuance to get your own attorney. If you make a mistake and lose you may have to pay the tenant's attorney fees.

Mediation

In some areas, mediation services are recommended or required before trial. At mediation, the parties are encouraged to resolve their differences. This may mean a planned date of departure for the tenant, or perhaps allowing the tenant to stay in the premises with a timetable for paying the back rent. However, in some cases, damage to the premises or animosity between the parties may make it impossible to continue the tenancy.

If a settlement is reached, it will be put in writing in the form of a *stipulation*, which is a written agreement that is filed with the court. If you merely dismiss your case as part of the settlement, you will have to start all over from scratch if the tenant again defaults.

Writ of Possession

Once your Final Judgment has been signed by the judge, if the tenant has still not vacated the premises, you must take a Writ of Possession (form 34), and one extra copy of it, to the clerk and pay the sheriff's fee for the eviction.

Regaining Possession

Different counties have different procedures for removing a tenant's possessions. Check with your local sheriff. In some cases, the sheriff stands by while the landlord removes the property. In such a case, the landlord would in effect be acting as a deputy sheriff and would be protected by law from the tenant.

In one case, when a sheriff came to deliver the Writ of Possession, the tenant was such a good talker he talked the sheriff out of executing the Writ of Possession. The sheriff called his office and a supervisor called the judge who said there was no motion pending to stay the writ. The sheriff still didn't execute the writ, but instead called another employee of the sheriff's department who called another judge to ask for a hearing. The landlord had to get an attorney and eventually the court found that there was no reason whatsoever for the deputy to fail to serve the writ as he was supposed to by law. He hinted that the sheriff should have called the sheriff department's attorney to learn that he was required by law to serve the writ. The tenant was ordered to pay at least part of the landlord's attorney fees.

If the personal property left on the premises appears to have been abandoned, it should be treated as explained in chapter 8.

Money Damages and Back Rent

Procedures for collecting money damages and back rent from a tenant are explained in the next chapter.

Tenant's Possible Defenses

A tenant who is behind in rent usually has one objective: to stay in the property rent-free as long as possible. Tenants and the lawyers provided to them at no charge by legal aid clinics (paid for by landlords' tax dollars) sometimes come up with creative, though ridiculous, defenses. Here is case law to help defeat their arguments.

Constitutionality

A tenant claims it is unconstitutional to have a quick eviction procedure and to require the tenant to pay the rent into the court before he or she is allowed to present any defenses. The U.S. Supreme Court says that such procedures can be constitutional. *Lindsey v. Normet*, 465 U.S. 56 (1972).

Security Deposit

A tenant says that he is not in default because the landlord has his security deposit which covers the default. Wrong. A security deposit is for a specific purpose at the end of the tenancy and does not cover current rent.

Amount Incorrect

A tenant disputes the amount of rent due. This is not a defense because, if any rent is due, landlord is entitled to eviction. However, if the amount stated in the three-day demand is wrong, the case may be dismissed.

Title

If a tenant files a written answer denying that the landlord has title, the action will be withdrawn from small claims court and transferred to district court for hearing (N.C.G.S. § 7A-223).

Fictitious Name

A tenant says that the landlord is using a fictitious name that has not been registered with the county. If the landlord actually is using an unregistered name, the case is abated until he complies with the statute. (For more information on registering a fictitious name, see *How to Start a Business in North Carolina*, by Jacqueline D.Stanley and Mark Warda, available through your local bookstore, or directly from Sphinx Publishing by calling 1-800-226-5291).

WAIVER BY ACCEPTANCE OF RENT

In a summary ejectment case based on the tenant's failure to pay rent, if the tenant files an answer alleging the tender of rent, it is proper for the magistrate to deny the landlord's request for a judgment ordering a tenant's eviction. *Hoover v. Crotts*, 232 N.C. 617, 61 S.E.2d 705 (1950).

REG. Z

A tenant says that the landlord has not complied with "Reg. Z," of the Code of Federal Regulations. This is a federal truth-in-lending requirement, which does not apply to the rental of property [12 CFR 226.1(c)(1)].

UNCONSCIONABILITY OF RENT

A tenant claims that the rent is *unconscionable*. This is a legal conclusion, and a tenant must state facts that would prove to the court that the rent is unconscionable.

INSUFFICIENT COMPLAINT

A tenant says that the landlord's complaint is not drawn properly and does not state a cause of action. The complaints included in this book include all elements necessary in a complaint. Landlord's are only required to be in "substantial conformity" with the rules regarding the format and content of summary ejectment complaints (N.C.G.S. § 7A-232).

MAINTENANCE OF PREMISES

A tenant says that the landlord has not complied with N.C.G.S. § 42-42, and that the tenant is withholding rent. This defense may not be raised because the law in North Carolina is clear: a tenant cannot withhold rent under these circumstances. A tenant's obligation to pay rent and a landlord's obligation to maintain the premises are not "mutually dependent" (N.C.G.S. 42-41).

EQUITABLE DEFENSES

There is a general rule that only the district court can hear "equitable matters." Tenants sometimes try to raise "equitable defenses" in an eviction case, in order to delay it by transferring it to district court. But as a practical matter, if this defense is raised in small claims court, the magistrate will reject it. The tenant will have an opportunity to appeal and have the case heard in district court.

RETALIATORY CONDUCT

A tenant says that he is being evicted in retaliation for some lawful action, and that this is illegal under N.C.G.S. § 42-37.1. This defense does not apply if the landlord is evicting the tenant for good cause, such as non-payment of rent, violation of the lease or reasonable rules, or violation of the landlord/tenant law.

Discovery A tenant wants more time in order to take *discovery*, which means to ask questions of the landlord and any witnesses under oath before a court reporter. This should not delay the case. The landlord should request that the discovery be completed quickly, and before the scheduled hearing date.

Jury Trial If the summary ejectment action is filed in District Court, either the landlord or tenant may request a jury trial. If the action is initially filed in small claims court, the magistrate will deny this request. The party requesting the jury trial can appeal and request a jury trial when the case is heard in District Court.

Attorney Busy or Unprepared The tenant's attorney may say that he or she just got on the case and needs time to prepare or has a busy schedule and is not available for trial for a month or so. This should not delay the case! If the tenant's attorney is unavailable, he shouldn't have taken the case. If the tenant has a lawyer, you should have one too.

Attorney's Fees for Dismissal When a tenant moves out of the property, the landlord sometimes dismisses his case. In some cases, the tenants have then claimed that they should have their attorney fees paid because they are the "prevailing party" in the case. But, if the landlord dismisses his case because there is no longer an issue, this does not make the tenant the prevailing party.

If a landlord is handling his own eviction, the landlord should not dismiss the case after the tenant moves. He should proceed to judgment, at least for the court costs and to be officially granted possession. If the landlord is represented by an attorney, he will have to weigh the costs.

Grievance Procedure In federally subsidized housing, the regulations require that tenants be given a grievance procedure in some evictions. However, where the tenant is a threat to the health and safety of other tenants or employees, Title 24 CFR, Chapter 9, § 966.51(a), states that such a grievance hearing is not required.

Tenant's Possible Countersuits

Another way tenants try to delay things is by filing a countersuit. This should not delay the eviction because both the original claim and the countersuit claim can be heard at the same time.

Exceeding Jurisdiction Since small claims court can only hear cases of amounts under $3,000, tenants sometimes try to claim over $3,000 in damages against the landlords. This way they hope to transfer the case to district court where it will drag out for a long time. In most cases, a claim of over $3,000 is clearly ridiculous and obviously intended as a delaying tactic. As a general rule, the magistrate will not allow the tenant to use this claim as a means of delay.

Negligence A landlord's failure to maintain the premises may be a breach of contract, but alone it is not actionable negligence.

Malicious Prosecution A malicious prosecution action cannot be brought in the same case as the original landlord's complaint. Malicious prosecution is a separate lawsuit that can be brought only if the landlord loses the original suit.

Moving Costs Tenants are not entitled to moving expenses after a lawful eviction.

Class Action Since the claims of each tenant will, in most cases, be different; they probably cannot counterclaim as a class action suit on behalf of all tenants in the building.

Abandonment after Dismissal

In some cases, the tenant will fight the eviction, have it dismissed on a technicality, and then move out of the unit. In such a situation, the judge may give you the right to refile the case to correct the error. However, if the tenant has vacated the premises, it won't be necessary to refile unless they owe you money for rent or damages.

TENANT'S APPEAL

A tenant has ten days from the date of the court's final judgment in which to file a notice of appeal. Tenant's can give notice of appeal in open court.

If the tenant files the appeal, they have twenty days after the judgment is entered to pay the cost of appeal to the clerk of court. Tenants who cannot afford the cost of appeal have ten days after the judgment is entered to take steps to be declared indigent.

If the tenant wishes to remain in the rental property, they have ten days after the entry of the judgment to pay a "stay of execution bond." The stay of execution bond includes rental payments as they become due, and an amount equal to prorated rent for the period between the date of judgment and the next rental payment date. Indigent tenants will not be required to pay the prorated rent, but they are required to pay the rent as it becomes due.

While the appeal case is waiting to be heard in district court, the landlord can ask the clerk to give him or her the rental payments as they become due. If the amount of rent is an issue on appeal, the clerk can give the landlord the undisputed portion.

TENANT'S BANKRUPTCY

If a tenant files bankruptcy, all legal actions against him or her must stop immediately. This provision is automatic from the moment the bankruptcy petition is filed (11 USC 362). If you take any action in court, seize the tenant's property, try to impose a landlord's lien, or use the security deposit for unpaid rent, you can be held in contempt of federal court. It is not necessary that you receive formal notice. Verbal notice is sufficient. If you do not believe the tenant, you should call the bankruptcy court to confirm the filing. The stay lasts until the debtor is discharged, the case is dismissed, the property is abandoned or voluntarily surrendered, or you obtain the permission of the bankruptcy court to proceed with the eviction.

Relief from Stay

The landlord may ask for the right to continue with the eviction by filing a Motion for Relief from Stay and paying the filing fee (which is currently $60). Within thirty days a hearing is held and it may be held by telephone. The motion is governed by Bankruptcy Rule 9014, and the requirements of how the tenant must be served are contained in Rule 7004. However, for such a hearing the services of an attorney are usually necessary.

Post-Filing Rent

The bankruptcy stay only applies to amounts owed to the landlord at the time of filing the bankruptcy. Therefore, the landlord can sue the tenant for eviction and rent owed for any time period ***after*** the filing, unless the bankruptcy trustee assumes the lease. The landlord can proceed during the bankruptcy without asking for relief from the automatic stay under three conditions. *In re Knight*, 8 B.R. 925 (D.C. Md. 1981):

1. The landlord can only sue for rent due after the filing.
2. The landlord cannot sue until the trustee rejects the lease. (If the trustee does not accept the lease within sixty days of the Order for Relief, then § 365(d)(1) provides that it is deemed rejected.)
3. The landlord must sue under the terms of the lease and may not treat the trustee's rejection as a breach.

In a Chapter 13 reorganization bankruptcy, the landlord should be paid the rent as it comes due.

Filing After Judgment

If the tenant filed bankruptcy after a judgment of eviction has been entered, there should be no problem lifting the automatic stay since the tenant has no interest in the property.

If your tenant files bankruptcy and you decide it is worth hiring a lawyer, you should locate an attorney who is experienced in bankruptcy work. Prior to the meeting with the attorney you should gather as much information as possible (type of bankruptcy filed, assets, liabilities, case number, etc.). This can be done by examining the tenant's file at the bankruptcy court.

LANDLORD'S APPEAL

If the landlord loses, he or she has the right to appeal the judgment. The desire to appeal the magistrate's decision may be stated in open court. The landlord also has twenty days after the entry of the judgment to the pay the cost of appeal.

GROUNDS

Our legal system allows one chance to bring a case to court. If you didn't prepare for your trial, or thought you wouldn't need a witness, and you lost; you don't have the right to try again. However, in certain limited circumstances, you may be able to have your case reviewed. These include:

- If the judge made a mistake in interpreting the law which applies to your case, it is grounds for reversal.
- If new evidence is discovered after the trial which could not have been discovered before the trial, a new trial might be granted (but this is not very common).

The following are ***not*** valid grounds for having a case reviewed on appeal:

- If one party lied at trial and that party was believed by the judge or jury, there is usually not much that can be done.
- There are certain other grounds for rehearing such as misconduct of an attorney or errors during the trial, but these matters are beyond the scope of this book.

Satisfaction of Judgment

If, after a judgment has been entered against the tenant, the tenant pays the amount due, it is the landlord's responsibility to notify the court clerk that the judgment has been satisfied. The exact procedure for doing this varies from county to county, so check with your clerk's office.

Money Damages and Back Rent 11

Trying to collect a judgment against a former tenant is usually not worth the time and expense. Most landlords are just glad to regain possession of the property. Tenants who don't pay rent usually don't own property that can be seized; and it is very difficult to garnish wages in North Carolina. However, occasionally former tenants come into money, and some landlords have been surprised many years later when called by a title insurance company who wants to pay off the judgment. Therefore, it is usually worthwhile to put a claim for back rent into an eviction complaint.

Landlords are entitled to receive money from tenants in the following instances:

- Tenant ended lease without paying rent. The landlord is entitled to the amount upon which the parties agreed.
- Tenant held over at the end of the lease and refuses to pay rent. The landlord is entitled to the "fair rental value" of the leased premises.
- Tenant damaged the rental premises.

Making a Claim

Landlords have two options when making a claim for money damages and back rent:

1. File a summary ejectment action which includes a claim for money owed. To make a claim against a tenant for back rent check the appropriate box on the Summary Ejectment Complaint (form 19).
2. File a separate lawsuit. This may be necessary if the claim for money owed exceeds the jurisdictional amount in small claims court. Also, if you want to expedite the tenant's departure, you should file the summary ejectment action first, and wait to file the claim for money owed.

Residential

In a residential eviction, if you have not included a demand for rent, the magistrate should allow you to amend the complaint while you are in the courtroom; but only if the tenant was personally served or properly served by certified or registered mail. If you forgot to ask for rent, did not get personal service, or the tenant moved out without the need for an eviction preceding, you can file a separate lawsuit for the rent owed. If the amount is less than $3,000 then the suit can be filed in small claims court.

Non-residential

In a non-residential tenancy, the lease may dictate what needs to be done before you can file a lawsuit.

Amount

Prorated Rent

Rent is uniformly prorated over the month. Therefore, if a landlord took possession of the dwelling unit for his own benefit, the tenant would be liable for rent only until he vacates the premises.

Late Fees

The North Carolina legislature (N.C.G.S. § 42-46) has established the following rules with respect to late fees:

- The late fee must be set out in the rental agreement
- The date the rent payment is due must be fixed
- The fee can't exceed $15.00 or five percent of the rental payment (whichever is greater)
- The fee can't be imposed until the rent is five or more days late
- The fee can only be imposed once for each late payment
- Landlords can't deduct late fees from subsequent payments, thereby making those payments late
- It is a violation of public policy for landlords and tenants to agree to terms contrary to these rules

INTEREST A landlord is entitled to interest on the rent from the day it is due until the date of the judgment.

DAMAGE TO THE PREMISES The landlord may sue the tenant for damage to the premises, but this does not include "normal wear and tear." (See page 30.)

OTHER LOSSES A landlord may make a claim against the tenant for other losses related to the damage or breach. Where a landlord lost rent while he was repairing the premises, he was allowed to claim this amount against the tenant.

HEARINGS

A landlord may request an eviction and a money judgment at the same hearing. If the tenant doesn't appear, it is still important that the final judgment for money damages state that the landlord is entitled to possession to be sure the tenant doesn't make trouble later. It is also important to bring documentation to support your claim for money damages.

Defenses

The fact that a landlord accepts rental payments after the entry of a summary eviction is not a plausible defense and will not prevent the landlord from gaining possession of the premises (N.C.G.S. § 42-30).

Liens

Pursuant to the North Carolina law [N.C.G.S. § 44A-2(E)], a landlord is given a lien on the property of the tenant which has been brought on the premises. Examples of the type of property for which the landlord may have a lien include: furniture, furnishings, trade fixtures, equipment, and other personal property.

The lien does not arise until after the occurrence of these two events:

1. Tenant has vacated the premises for twenty-one or more days after the paid rental period has ended
2. The landlord has a lawful claim for damages against the tenant

The law in this area is very complicated. Before attempting to enforce a landlord's lien, be sure to consult an attorney.

Distress for Rent and Replevin

In nonresidential tenancies, there is a procedure called *distress for rent.* This involves posting a bond, having the sheriff levy upon the tenant's property, and forbidding the tenant to move it from the premises.

There is also a procedure called *replevin* by which the property of the tenant may be sold to pay the rent owed to the landlord.

Both of these procedures are complicated and will require the assistance of an attorney.

Self Service Storage Space 12

Applicability

The provisions contained in N.C.G.S., Chapter 42, which contains the landlord/tenant law, does not apply to renting individual storage space to tenants who have access for storing and removing personal property. The law is clear that no occupant shall use a self-service storage facility for residential purposes.

If an owner issues a warehouse receipt or other receipt for property in storage, the relationship of the parties is governed by N.C.G.S., Chapter 25, Article 7. All other self-storage arrangements are governed by N.C.G.S. §§ 44A-40 to 44A-46.

Withholding Access

After rent is fifteen days overdue, the owner of a self-storage facility may withhold access to the property located in the unit without giving notice (N.C.G.S. § 44A-43).

LIENS

The owner of a self-storage facility has a lien for rent, labor, or other charges on the property in the unit. It does not matter whose property it is, the lien attaches to any property in the unit on the date it is brought to the facility.

In order to assert the lien, a notice must first be sent by registered mail to the last-known address of the occupant. The notice must specifically state:

- That the lien is being asserted against the specific property of the lienor (owner)
- That the lien is being asserted for rental charges at the self-storage facility
- The amount of the lien
- The lienor intends to sell or dispose of the property in order to satisfy the lien

The notice must also include the following information:

- A general description of the property
- A statement regarding the right to a hearing
- A statement that the occupant has ten days to request a hearing

After the ten days have passed, an advertisement for the sale or other disposition (which could mean to throw away) must be published once a week for two consecutive weeks in a newspaper of general circulation in the area. The property of several tenants may be listed in one ad if one sale will be held. The ad must include:

- A statement that the items are being sold pursuant to the assertion of a lien for rental at the self-storage facility.
- The address of the self-service storage facility and the name of the occupant

- ☛ The time, place, date, and manner of the sale or other disposition (the sale or other disposition must take place not sooner than twenty days after the first publication)

The sale can take place on any day, other than Sunday, between the hours of 10 A.M. and 4 P.M. It must be held at the self-storage facility or at a location near to where the property is stored. The sale must take place in the county where the agreement to store the property was made.

The final disposition must conform to the terms in the ad and must be in a "commercially reasonable manner," which, according to another law, means the property may be sold in one lot, or individually if that is more reasonable, and the owner may buy at the sale.

Any time before the sale, the tenant may redeem the property by paying the money due plus the expenses in preparing for the sale.

The rights of purchasers at the sale, and of the landlord, to the proceeds are complicated by the laws of lien priority. For larger, expensive items of personal property, such as vehicles and machinery, a search for liens should be made through the Department of Motor Vehicles, the County Register of Deeds office, or the Secretary of State UCC division. Prior liens of this type would remain on the property.

However, in most cases, the property is inexpensive personal items which would not have liens against it, and no future claims can be expected.

If an owner fails to follow the rules regarding enforcing storage liens, they can be fined $100 and ordered to pay reasonable attorney fees.

Appendix A
North Carolina Statutes

This appendix includes Chapter 42 of the North Carolina General Statutes, which applies to landlord/tenant relationships. Below you will find a listing of the various sections of Chapter 42, with the full text beginning on page 97.

CHAPTER 42
Landlord and Tenant

ARTICLE 1.
General Provisions.

§ 42-1. Lessor and lessee not partners.

§ 42-2. Attornment unnecessary on conveyance of reversions, etc.

§ 42-3. Term forfeited for nonpayment of rent.

§ 42-4. Recovery for use and occupation.

§ 42-5. Rent apportioned, where lease terminated by death.

§ 42-6. Rents, annuities, etc., apportioned, where right to payment terminated by death.

§ 42-7. In lieu of emblements, farm lessee holds out year, with rents apportioned.

§ 42-8. Grantees of reversion and assigns of lease have reciprocal rights under covenants.

§ 42-9. Agreement to rebuild, how construed in case of fire.

§ 42-10. Tenant not liable for accidental damage.

§ 42-11. Willful destruction by tenant misdemeanor.

§ 42-12. Lessee may surrender, where building destroyed or damaged.

§ 42-13. Wrongful surrender to other than landlord misdemeanor.

§ 42-14. Notice to quit in certain tenancies.

§ 42-14.1. Rent control.

§ 42-14.2. Death, illness, or conviction of certain crimes not a material fact.

ARTICLE 2.
Agricultural Tenancies.

§ 42-15. Landlord's lien on crops for rents, advances, etc.; enforcement.

§ 42-15.1. Landlord's lien on crop insurance for rents, advances, etc.; enforcement.

§ 42-16. Rights of tenants.

§ 42-17. Action to settle dispute between parties.

§ 42-18. Tenant's undertaking on continuance or appeal.

§ 42-19. Crops delivered to landlord on his undertaking.

§ 42-20. Crops sold, if neither party gives undertaking.

§ 42-21. Tenant's crop not subject to execution against landlord.

§ 42-22. Unlawful seizure by landlord or removal by tenant misdemeanor.

§ 42-22.1. Failure of tenant to account for sales under tobacco marketing cards.

§ 42-23. Terms of agricultural tenancies in certain counties.

ARTICLE 1.

General Provisions.

§ 42-1. Lessor and lessee not partners. No lessor of property, merely by reason that he is to receive as rent or compensation for its use a share of the proceeds or net profits of the business in which it is employed, or any other uncertain consideration, shall be held a partner of the lessee.

§ 42-2. Attornment unnecessary on conveyance of reversions, etc. Every conveyance of any rent, reversion, or remainder in lands, tenements or hereditaments, otherwise sufficient, shall be deemed complete without attornment by the holders of particular estates in said lands: Provided, no holder of a particular estate shall be prejudiced by any act done by him as holding under his grantor, without notice of such conveyance.

§ 42-3. Term forfeited for nonpayment of rent. In all verbal or written leases of real property of any kind in which is fixed a definite time for the payment of the rent reserved therein, there shall be implied a forfeiture of the term upon failure to pay the rent within 10 days after a demand is made by the lessor or his agent on said lessee for all past-due rent, and the lessor may forthwith enter and dispossess the tenant without having declared such forfeiture or reserved the right of reentry in the lease.

§ 42-4. Recovery for use and occupation. When any person occupies land of another by the permission of such other, without any express agreement for rent, or upon a parol lease which is void, the landlord may recover a reasonable compensation for such occupation, and if by such parol lease a certain rent was reserved, such reservation may be received as evidence of the value of the occupation.

§ 42-5. Rent apportioned, where lease terminated by death. If a lease of land, in which rent is reserved, payable at the end of the year or other certain period of time, is determined by the death of any person during one of the periods in which the rent was growing due, the lessor or his personal representative may recover a part of the rent which becomes due after the death, proportionate to the part of the period elapsed before the death, subject to all just allowances; and if any security was given for such rent it shall be apportioned in like manner.

§ 42-6. Rents, annuities, etc., apportioned, where right to payment terminated by death. In all cases where rents, rent charges, annuities, pensions, dividends, or any other payments of any description, are made payable at fixed periods to successive owners under any instrument, or by any will, and where the right of any owner to receive payment is terminable by a death or other uncertain event, and where such right so terminates during a period in which a payment is growing due, the payment becoming due next after such terminating event shall be apportioned among the successive owners according to the parts of such periods elapsing before and after the terminating event.

§ 42-7. In lieu of emblements, farm lessee holds out year, with rents apportioned. When any lease for years of any land let for farming on which a rent is reserved determines during a current year of the tenancy, by the happening of any uncertain event determining the estate of the lessor, or by a sale of said land under any mortgage or deed of trust, the tenant in lieu of emblements shall continue his occupation to the end of such current year, and shall then give up such possession to the succeeding owner of the land, and shall pay to such succeeding owner a part of the rent accrued since the last payment became due, proportionate to the part of the period of payment elapsing after the termination of the estate of the lessor to the giving up such possession; and the tenant in such case shall be entitled to a reasonable compensation for the tillage and seed of any crop not gathered at the expiration of such current year from the person succeeding to the possession.

§ 42-8. Grantees of reversion and assigns of lease have reciprocal rights under covenants. The grantee in every conveyance of reversion in lands, tenements or hereditaments has the like advantages and remedies by action or entry against the holders of particular estates in such real property, and their assigns, for nonpayment of rent, and for the nonperformance of other conditions and agreements contained in the instruments by the tenants of such particular estates, as the grantor or lessor or his heirs might have; and the holders of such particular estates, and their assigns, have the like advantages and remedies against the grantee of the reversion, or any part thereof, for any conditions and agreements contained in such instruments, as they might have had against the grantor or his lessors or his heirs.

§ 42-9. Agreement to rebuild, how construed in case of fire. An agreement in a lease to repair a demised house shall not be construed to bind the contracting party to rebuild or repair in case the house shall be destroyed or damaged to more than one half of its value, by accidental fire not occurring from the want of ordinary diligence on his part.

§ 42-10. Tenant not liable for accidental damage. A tenant for life, or years, or for a less term, shall not be liable for damage occurring on the demised premises accidentally, and notwithstanding reasonable diligence on his part, unless he so contract.

§ 42-11. Willful destruction by tenant misdemeanor. If any tenant shall, during his term or after its expiration, willfully and unlawfully demolish, destroy, deface, injure or damage any tenement house, uninhabited house or other outhouse, belonging to his landlord or upon his premises by removing parts thereof or by burning, or in any other manner, or shall unlawfully and willfully burn, destroy, pull down, injure or remove any fence, wall or other inclosure or any part thereof, built or standing upon the premises of such landlord, or shall willfully and unlawfully cut down or destroy any timber, fruit, shade or ornamental tree belonging to said landlord, he shall be guilty of a Class 1 misdemeanor.

§ 42-12. Lessee may surrender, where building destroyed or damaged. If a demised house, or other building, is destroyed during the term, or so much damaged that it cannot be made reasonably fit for the purpose for which it was hired, except at an expense exceeding one year's rent of the premises, and the damage or destruction occur without negligence on the part of the lessee or his agents or servants, and there is no agreement in the lease respecting repairs, or providing for such a case, and the use of the house damaged or destroyed was the main inducement to the hiring, the lessee may surrender his estate in the demised premises by a writing to that effect delivered or tendered to the landlord within 10 days from the damage or destruction, and by paying or tendering at the same time all rent in arrears, and a part of the rent growing due at the time of the damage or destruction, proportionate to the time between the last period of payment and the occurrence of the damage or destruction, and the lessee shall be thenceforth discharged from all rent accruing afterwards; but not from any other agreement in the lease. This section shall not apply if a contrary intention appear from the lease.

§ 42-13. Wrongful surrender to other than landlord misdemeanor. Any tenant or lessee of lands who shall willfully, wrongfully and with intent to defraud the landlord or lessor, give up the possession of the rented or leased premises to any person other than his landlord or lessor, shall be guilty of a Class 1 misdemeanor.

§ 42-14. Notice to quit in certain tenancies. A tenancy from year to year may be terminated by a notice to quit given one month or more before the end of the current year of the tenancy; a tenancy from month to month by a like notice of seven days; a tenancy from week to week, of two days. Provided, however, where the tenancy involves only the rental of a space for a manufactured home as defined in G.S. 143-143.9(6), a notice to quit must be given at least 30 days before the end of the current rental period, regardless of the term of the tenancy.

§ 42-14.1. Rent control. No county or city as defined by G.S. 160A-1 may enact, maintain, or enforce any ordinance or resolution which regulates the amount of rent to be charged for privately owned, single- family or multiple unit residential or commercial rental property. This section shall not be construed as prohibiting any county or city, or any authority created by a county or city for that purpose, from:

(1) Regulating in any way property belonging to that city, county, or authority;
(2) Entering into agreements with private persons which regulate the amount of rent charged for subsidized rental properties; or
(3) Enacting ordinances or resolutions restricting rent for properties assisted with Community Development Block Grant Funds.

§ 42-14.2. Death, illness, or conviction of certain crimes not a material fact. In offering real property for rent or lease it shall not be deemed a material fact that the real property was occupied previously by a person who died or had a serious illness while occupying the property or that a person convicted of any crime for which registration is required by Article 27A of Chapter 14 of the General Statutes occupies, occupied, or resides near the property; provided, however, that no landlord or lessor may knowingly make a false statement regarding any such fact.

ARTICLE 2.

Agricultural Tenancies.

§ 42-15. Landlord's lien on crops for rents, advances, etc.; enforcement. When lands are rented or leased by agreement, written or oral, for agricultural purposes, or are cultivated by a cropper, unless otherwise agreed between the parties to the lease or agreement, any and all crops raised on said lands shall be deemed and held to be vested in possession of the lessor or his assigns at all times, until the rents for said lands are paid and until all the stipulations contained in the lease or agreement are performed, or damages in lieu thereof paid to the lessor or his assigns, and until said party or his assigns is paid for all advancements made and expenses incurred in making and saving said crops.

This lien shall be preferred to all other liens, and the lessor or his assigns is entitled, against the lessee or cropper, or the assigns of either, who removes the crop or any part thereof from the lands without the consent of the lessor or his assigns, or against any other person who may get possession of said crop or any part thereof, to the remedies given in an action upon a claim for the delivery of personal property.

Provided, that when advances have been made by the federal government or any of its agencies, to any tenant or tenants on lands under the control of any guardian, executor and/or administrator for the purpose of enabling said tenant or tenants to plant, cultivate and harvest crops grown on said land, the said guardian, executor, and/or administrator may waive the above lien in favor of the federal government, or any of its agencies, making said advances.

§ 42-15.1. Landlord's lien on crop insurance for rents, advances, etc.; enforcement. Where lands are rented or leased by agreement, written or oral, for agricultural purposes, or are cultivated by a cropper, unless otherwise agreed between the parties to the lease or agreement, the landlord or his assigns shall have a lien on all the insurance procured by the tenant or cropper on the crops raised on the lands leased or rented to the extent of any rents due or advances made to the tenant or cropper.

The lien provided herein shall be preferred to all other liens on said insurance, and the landlord or his assigns shall be entitled to all the remedies at law for the enforcement of the lien.

§ 42-16. Rights of tenants. When the lessor or his assigns gets the actual possession of the crop or any part thereof otherwise than by the mode prescribed in G.S. 42-15, and refuses or neglects, upon a notice, written or oral, of five days, given by the lessee or cropper or the assigns of either, to make a fair division of said crop, or to pay over to such lessee or cropper or the assigns of either, such part thereof as he may be entitled to under the lease or agreement, then and in that case the lessee or cropper or the assigns of either is entitled to the remedies against the lessor or his assigns given in an action upon a claim for the delivery of personal property to recover such part of the crop as he, in law and according to the lease or agreement, may be entitled to. The amount or quantity of such crop claimed by said lessee or cropper or the assigns of either, together with a statement of the grounds upon which it is claimed, shall be fully set forth in an affidavit at the beginning of the action.

§ 42-17. Action to settle dispute between parties. When any controversy arises between the parties, and neither party avails himself of the provisions of this Chapter, it is competent for either party to proceed at once to have the matter determined in the appropriate trial division of the General Court of Justice.

§ 42-18. Tenant's undertaking on continuance or appeal. In case there is a continuance or an appeal from the magistrate's decision to the district court, the lessee or cropper, or the assigns of either, shall be allowed to retain possession of said property upon his giving an undertaking to the lessor or his assigns, or the adverse party, in a sum double the amount of the claim, if such claim does not amount to more than the value of such property, otherwise to double the value of such property, with good and sufficient surety, to be approved by the magistrate or the clerk of the superior court, conditioned for the faithful payment to the adverse party of such damages as he shall recover in said action.

§ 42-19. Crops delivered to landlord on his undertaking. In case the lessee or cropper, or the assigns of either, at the time of the appeal or continuance mentioned in G.S. 42-18, fails to give the undertaking therein required, then the sheriff or other lawful officer shall deliver the property into the actual possession of the lessor or his assigns, upon the lessor or his assigns giving to the adverse party an undertaking in double the amount of said property, to be justified as required in G.S. 42-18, conditioned for the forthcoming of such property, or the value thereof, in case judgment is pronounced against him.

§ 42-20. Crops sold, if neither party gives undertaking. If neither party gives the undertaking described in G.S. 42-18 and 42-19, it is the duty of the clerk of the superior court to issue an order to the sheriff, or other lawful officer, directing him to take into his possession all of said property, or so much thereof as may be necessary to satisfy the claimant's demand and costs, and to sell the same under the rules and regulations prescribed by law for the sale of personal property under execution, and to hold the proceeds thereof subject to the decision of the court upon the issue or issues pending between the parties.

§ 42-21. Tenant's crop not subject to execution against landlord. Whenever servants and laborers in agriculture shall by their contracts, oral or written, be entitled, for wages, to a part of the crops cultivated by them, such part shall not be subject to sale under executions against their employers, or the owners of the land cultivated.

§ 42-22. Unlawful seizure by landlord or removal by tenant misdemeanor. If any landlord shall unlawfully, willfully, knowingly and without process of law, and unjustly seize the crop of his tenant when there is nothing due him, he shall be guilty of a Class 1 misdemeanor. If any lessee or cropper, or the assigns of either, or any other person, shall remove a crop, or any part thereof, from land without the consent of the lessor or his assigns, and without giving him or his agent five days' notice of such intended removal, and before satisfying all the liens held by the lessor or his assigns, on said crop, he shall be guilty of a Class 1 misdemeanor.

§ 42-22.1. Failure of tenant to account for sales under tobacco marketing cards. Any tenant or share cropper having possession of a tobacco marketing card issued by any agency of the State or federal government who sells tobacco authorized to be sold thereby and fails to account to his landlord, to the extent of the net proceeds of such sale or sales, for all liens, rents, advances, or other claims held by his landlord against the tobacco or the proceeds of the sale of such tobacco, shall be guilty of a Class 1 misdemeanor.

§ 42-23. Terms of agricultural tenancies in certain counties. All agricultural leases and contracts hereafter made between landlord and tenant for a period of one year or from year to year, whether such tenant pay a specified rental or share in the crops grown, such year shall be from December first to December first, and such period of time shall constitute a year for agricultural tenancies in lieu of the law and custom heretofore prevailing, namely from

January first to January first. In all cases of such tenancies a notice to quit of one month as provided in G.S. 42-14 shall be applicable. If on account of illness or any other good cause, the tenant is unable to harvest all the crops grown on lands leased by him for any year prior to the termination of his lease contract on December first, he shall have a right to return to the premises vacated by him at any time prior to December thirty-first of said year, for the purpose only of harvesting and dividing the remaining crops so ungathered. But he shall have no right to use the houses or outbuildings or that part of the lands from which the crops have been harvested prior to the termination of the tenant year, as defined in this section.

This section shall only apply to the counties of Alamance, Anson, Ashe, Bladen, Brunswick, Columbus, Craven, Cumberland, Duplin, Edgecombe, Gaston, Greene, Hoke, Jones, Lenoir, Lincoln, Montgomery, Onslow, Pender, Person, Pitt, Robeson, Sampson, Wayne and Yadkin.

§ 42-24. Turpentine and lightwood leases. This Chapter shall apply to all leases or contracts to lease turpentine trees, or use lightwood for purposes of making tar, and the parties thereto shall be fully subject to the provisions and penalties of this Chapter.

§ 42-25. Mining and timberland leases. If in a lease of land for mining, or of timbered land for the purpose of manufacturing the timber into goods, rent is reserved, and if it is agreed in the lease that the minerals, timber or goods, or any portion thereof, shall not be removed until the payment of the rent, in such case the lessor shall have the rights and be entitled to the remedy given by this Chapter.

ARTICLE 2A.

Ejectment of Residential Tenants.

§ 42-25.6. Manner of ejectment of residential tenants. It is the public policy of the State of North Carolina, in order to maintain the public peace, that a residential tenant shall be evicted, dispossessed or otherwise constructively or actually removed from his dwelling unit only in accordance with the procedure prescribed in Article 3 or Article 7 of this Chapter.

§ 42-25.7. Distress and distraint not permitted. It is the public policy of the State of North Carolina that distress and distraint are prohibited and that landlords of residential rental property shall have rights concerning the personal property of their residential tenants only in accordance with G.S. 42-25.9(d), 42-25.9(g), 42-25.9(h), or 42-36.2.

§ 42-25.8. Contrary lease provisions. Any lease or contract provision contrary to this Article shall be void as against public policy.

§ 42-25.9. Remedies.

(a) If any lessor, landlord, or agent removes or attempts to remove a tenant from a dwelling unit in any manner contrary to this Article, the tenant shall be entitled to recover possession or to terminate his lease and the lessor, landlord or agent shall be liable to the tenant for damages caused by the tenant's removal or attempted removal. Damages in any action brought by a tenant under this Article shall be limited to actual damages as in an action for trespass or conversion and shall not include punitive damages, treble damages or damages for emotional distress.

(b) If any lessor, landlord, or agent seizes possession of or interferes with a tenant's access to a tenant's or household member's personal property in any manner not in accordance with G.S. 42-25.9(d), 42-25.9(g), 42-25.9(h), or 42-36.2 the tenant or household member shall be entitled to recover possession of his personal property or compensation for the value of the personal property, and, in any action brought by a tenant or household member under this Article, the landlord shall be liable to the tenant or household member for actual damages, but not including punitive damages, treble damages or damages for emotional distress.

(c) The remedies created by this section are supplementary to all existing common-law and statutory rights and remedies.

(d) If any tenant abandons personal property of five hundred dollar ($500.00) value or less in the demised premises, or fails to remove such property at the time of execution of a writ of possession in an action for summary ejectment, the landlord may, as an alternative to the procedures provided in G.S. 42-25.9(g), 42-25.9(h), or 42-36.2, deliver the property into the custody of a nonprofit organization regularly providing free or at a nominal price clothing and household furnishings to people in need, upon that organization agreeing to identify and separately store the property for 30 days and to release the property to the tenant at no charge within the 30-day period. A landlord electing to use this procedure shall immediately post at the demised premises a notice containing the name and address of the property recipient, post the same notice for 30 days or more at the place where rent is received, and send the same notice by first-class mail to the tenant at the tenant's last known address. Provided, however, that the notice shall not include a description of the property.

(e) For purposes of subsection (d), personal property shall be deemed abandoned if the landlord finds evidence that clearly shows the premises has been voluntarily vacated after the paid rental period has expired and the landlord has no notice of a disability that caused the vacancy. A presumption of abandonment shall arise 10 or more days after the landlord has posted conspicuously a notice of suspected abandonment both inside and outside the premises and has received no response from the tenant.

(f) Any nonprofit organization agreeing to receive personal property under subsection (d) shall not be liable to the owner for a disposition of such property provided that the property has been separately identified and stored for release to the owner for a period of 30 days.

(g) Ten days after being placed in lawful possession by execution of a writ of possession, a landlord may throw away, dispose of, or sell all items of personal property remaining on the premises. During the 10-day period after being placed in lawful possession by execution of a writ of possession, a landlord may move for storage purposes, but shall not throw away, dispose of, or sell any items of personal property remaining on the premises unless otherwise provided for in this Chapter. Upon the tenant's request prior to the expiration of the 10-day period, the landlord shall release possession of the property to the tenant during regular business hours or at a time agreed upon. If the landlord elects to sell the property at public or private sale, the landlord shall give written notice to the tenant by first-class mail to the tenant's last known address at least seven days prior to the day of the sale. The seven-day notice of sale may run concurrently with the 10-day period which allows the tenant to request possession of the property. The written notice shall state the date, time, and place of the sale, and that any surplus of proceeds from the sale, after payment of unpaid rents, damages, storage fees, and sale costs, shall be disbursed to the tenant, upon request, within 10 days after the sale, and will thereafter be delivered to the government of the county in which the rental property is located. Upon the tenant's request prior to the day of sale, the landlord shall release possession of the property to the tenant during regular business hours or at a time agreed upon. The landlord may apply the proceeds of the sale to the unpaid rents, damages, storage fees, and sale costs. Any surplus from the sale shall be disbursed to the tenant, upon request, within 10 days of the sale and shall thereafter be delivered to the government of the county in which the rental property is located.

(h) If the total value of all property remaining on the premises at the time of execution of a writ of possession in an action for summary ejectment is less than one hundred dollars ($100.00), then the property shall be deemed abandoned five days after the time of execution, and the landlord may throw away or dispose of the property. Upon the tenant's request prior to the expiration of the five-day period, the landlord shall release possession of the property to the tenant during regular business hours or at a time agreed upon.

ARTICLE 3.

Summary Ejectment.

§ 42-26. Tenant holding over may be dispossessed in certain cases. Any tenant or lessee of any house or land, and the assigns under the tenant or legal representatives of such tenant or lessee, who holds over and continues in the possession of the demised premises, or any part thereof, without the permission of the landlord, and after demand made for its surrender, may be removed from such premises in the manner hereinafter prescribed in any of the following cases:

(1) When a tenant in possession of real estate holds over after his term has expired.

(2) When the tenant or lessee, or other person under him, has done or omitted any act by which, according to the stipulations of the lease, his estate has ceased.

(3) When any tenant or lessee of lands or tenements, who is in arrears for rent or has agreed to cultivate the demised premises and to pay a part of the crop to be made thereon as rent, or who has given to the lessor a lien on such crop as a security for the rent, deserts the demised premises, and leaves them unoccupied and uncultivated.

§ 42-27. Local: Refusal to perform contract ground for dispossession. When any tenant or cropper who enters into a contract for the rental of land for the current or ensuing year willfully neglects or refuses to perform the terms of his contract without just cause, he shall forfeit his right of possession to the premises. This section applies only to the following counties: Alamance, Alexander, Alleghany, Anson, Ashe, Beaufort, Bertie, Bladen, Brunswick, Burke, Cabarrus, Camden, Carteret, Caswell, Chatham, Chowan, Cleveland, Columbus, Craven, Cumberland, Currituck, Davidson, Duplin, Edgecombe, Forsyth, Franklin, Gaston, Gates, Greene, Guilford, Halifax, Harnett, Hertford, Hoke, Hyde, Jackson, Johnston, Jones, Lee, Lenoir, Martin, Mecklenburg, Montgomery, Moore, Nash, Northampton, Onslow, Pasquotank, Pender, Perquimans, Pitt, Polk, Randolph, Robeson, Rockingham, Rowan, Rutherford, Sampson, Stokes, Surry, Swain, Tyrrell, Union, Wake, Warren, Washington, Wayne, Wilson, Yadkin.

§ 42-28. Summons issued by clerk. When the lessor or his assignee files a complaint pursuant to G.S. 42-26 or 42-27, and asks to be put in possession of the leased premises, the clerk of superior court shall issue a summons requiring the defendant to appear at a certain time and place not to exceed seven days from the issuance of the summons, excluding weekends and legal holidays, to answer the complaint. The plaintiff may claim rent in arrears, and damages for the occupation of the premises since the cessation of the estate of the lessee, not to exceed the jurisdictional amount established by G.S. 7A-210(1), but if he omits to make such claim, he shall not be prejudiced thereby in any other action for their recovery.

§ **42-29. Service of summons.** The officer receiving the summons shall mail a copy of the summons and complaint to the defendant no later than the end of the next business day or as soon as practicable at the defendant's last known address in a stamped addressed envelope provided by the plaintiff to the action. The officer may, within five days of the issuance of the summons, attempt to telephone the defendant requesting that the defendant either personally visit the officer to accept service, or schedule an appointment for the defendant to receive delivery of service from the officer. If the officer does not attempt to telephone the defendant or the attempt is unsuccessful or does not result in service to the defendant, the officer shall make at least one visit to the place of abode of the defendant within five days of the issuance of the summons at a time reasonably calculated to find the defendant at the place of abode to attempt personal delivery of service. He then shall deliver a copy of the summons together with a copy of the complaint to the defendant, or leave copies thereof at the defendant's dwelling house or usual place of abode with some person of suitable age and discretion then residing therein. If such service cannot be made the officer shall affix copies to some conspicuous part of the premises claimed and make due return showing compliance with this section.

§ **42-30. Judgment by confession or where plaintiff has proved case.** The summons shall be returned according to its tenor, and if on its return it appears to have been duly served, and if the plaintiff proves his case by a preponderance of the evidence, or the defendant admits the allegations of the complaint, the magistrate shall give judgment that the defendant be removed from, and the plaintiff be put in possession of, the demised premises; and if any rent or damages for the occupation of the premises after the cessation of the estate of the lessee, not exceeding the jurisdictional amount established by G.S. 7A- 210(1), be claimed in the oath of the plaintiff as due and unpaid, the magistrate shall inquire thereof, and give judgment as he may find the fact to be.

§ **42-31. Trial by magistrate.** If the defendant by his answer denies any material allegation in the oath of the plaintiff, the magistrate shall hear the evidence and give judgment as he shall find the facts to be.

§ **42-32. Damages assessed to trial.** On appeal to the district court, the jury trying issues joined shall assess the damages of the plaintiff for the detention of his possession to the time of the trial in that court; and, if the jury finds that the detention was wrongful and that the appeal was without merit and taken for the purpose of delay, the plaintiff, in addition to any other damages allowed, shall be entitled to the amount of rent in arrears, or which may have accrued, to the time of trial in the district court. Judgment for the rent in arrears and for the damages assessed may, on motion, be rendered against the sureties to the appeal.

§ **42-33. Rent and costs tendered by tenant.** If, in any action brought to recover the possession of demised premises upon a forfeiture for the nonpayment of rent, the tenant, before judgment given in such action, pays or tenders the rent due and the costs of the action, all further proceedings in such action shall cease. If the plaintiff further prosecutes his action, and the defendant pays into court for the use of the plaintiff a sum equal to that which shall be found to be due, and the costs, to the time of such payment, or to the time of a tender and refusal, if one has occurred, the defendant shall recover from the plaintiff all subsequent costs; the plaintiff shall be allowed to receive the sum paid into court for his use, and the proceedings shall be stayed.

§ **42-34. Undertaking on appeal and order staying execution.**

(a) Upon appeal to the district court, either party may demand that the case be tried at the first session of the court after the appeal is docketed, but the presiding judge, in his discretion, may first try any pending case in which the rights of the parties or the public demand it. If the case has not been previously continued in district court, the court shall continue the case for an appropriate period of time if any party initiates discovery or files a motion to allow further pleadings pursuant to G.S. 7A-220 or G.S. 7A-229, or for summary judgment pursuant to Rule 56 of the Rules of Civil Procedure.

(b) During an appeal to district court, it shall be sufficient to stay execution of a judgment for ejectment if the defendant appellant pays to the clerk of superior court any rent in arrears as determined by the magistrate and signs an undertaking that he or she will pay into the office of the clerk of superior court the amount of the contract rent as it becomes due periodically after the judgment was entered and, where applicable, comply with subdivision (c) below. Provided however, when the magistrate makes a finding in the record, based on evidence presented in court, that there is an actual dispute as to the amount of rent in arrears that is due and the magistrate specifies the specific amount of rent in arrears in dispute, in order to stay execution of a judgment for ejectment, the defendant appellant shall not be required to pay to the clerk of superior court the amount of rent in arrears found by the magistrate to be in dispute, even if the magistrate's judgment includes this amount in the amount of rent found to be in arrears. If a defendant appellant appeared at the hearing before the magistrate and the magistrate found an amount of rent in arrears that was not in dispute, and if an attorney representing the defendant appellant on appeal to the district court signs a pleading stating that there is evidence of an actual dispute as to the amount of rent in arrears, then the defendant appellant shall not be required to pay the rent in arrears alleged to be in dispute to stay execution of a judgment for ejectment pending appeal. Any magistrate, clerk, or district court judge shall order stay of execution upon the defendant appellant's paying the undisputed rent in arrears to the clerk and signing the undertaking.If either party disputes the amount of the payment or the due date in the undertaking, the aggrieved party may move for modification of the terms of the undertaking before the clerk of superior court or the district court. Upon such motion and upon notice to all interested parties, the clerk or court shall hold a hearing and determine what modifications, if any, are appropriate.

(c) In an ejectment action based upon alleged nonpayment of rent where the judgment is entered more than five working days before the day when the next rent will be due under the lease, the appellant shall make an additional undertaking to stay execution pending appeal. Such additional undertaking shall be the payment of the prorated rent for the days between the day that the judgment was entered and the next day when the rent will be due under the lease.

(c1) Notwithstanding the provisions of subsection (b) of this section, an indigent defendant appellant, as set forth in G.S. 1-110, who prosecutes his or her appeal as an indigent and who meets the requirement of G.S. 1-288 shall pay the amount of the contract rent as it becomes periodically due as set forth in subsection (b) of this section, but shall not be required to pay rent in arrears as set forth in subsection (b) of this section in order to stay execution pending appeal.

(d) The undertaking by the appellant and the order staying execution may be substantially in the following form:

"State of North Carolina,

"County of

" , Plaintiff

vs.	Bond to
" , Defendant	Stay Execution
	On Appeal to
	District Court

"Now comes the defendant in the above entitled action and respectfully shows the court that judgment for summary ejectment was entered against the defendant and for the plaintiff on the.......... day of ...., 19..., by the Magistrate. Defendant has appealed the judgment to the District Court.

"Pursuant to the terms of the lease between plaintiff and defendant, defendant is obligated to pay rent in the amount of $...... per ....., due on the ..... day of each ......

"Where the payment of rent in arrears or an additional undertaking is required by G.S. 42-34, the defendant hereby tenders $...... to the Court as required.

"Defendant hereby undertakes to pay the periodic rent hereinafter due according to the aforesaid terms of the lease and moves the Court to stay execution on the judgment for summary ejectment until this matter is heard on appeal by the District Court.

"This the .... day of........, 19.....

Defendant

"Upon execution of the above bond, execution on said judgment for summary ejectment is hereby stayed until the action is heard on appeal in the District Court. If defendant fails to make any rental payment to the clerk's office within five days of the due date, upon application of the plaintiff, the stay of execution shall dissolve and the sheriff may dispossess the defendant.

"This .... day of ...., 19.....

Assistant Clerk of Superior Court."

(e) Upon application of the plaintiff, the clerk of superior court shall pay to the plaintiff any amount of the rental payments paid by the defendant into the clerk's office which are not claimed by the defendant in any pleadings.

(f) If the defendant fails to make a payment within five days of the due date according to the undertaking and order staying execution, the clerk, upon application of the plaintiff, shall issue execution on the judgment for possession.

(g) When it appears by stipulation executed by all of the parties or by final order of the court that the appeal has been resolved, the clerk of court shall disburse any accrued moneys of the undertaking remaining in the clerk's office according to the terms of the stipulation or order.

§ 42-34.1. Rent pending execution of judgment; post bond pending appeal.

(a) If the judgment in district court is against the defendant appellant and the defendant appellant does not appeal the judgment, the defendant appellant shall pay rent to the plaintiff for the time the defendant appellant remains in possession of the premises after the judgment is given. Rent shall be prorated if the judgment is executed before the day rent would become due under the terms of the lease. The clerk of court shall disperse any rent in arrears paid by the defendant appellant in accordance with a stipulation executed by all parties or, if there is no stipulation, in accordance with the judge's order.

(b) If the judgment in district court is against the defendant appellant and the defendant appellant appeals the judgment, it shall be sufficient to stay execution of the judgment if the defendant appellant posts a bond as provided in G.S. 42-34(b). If the defendant appellant fails to perfect the appeal or the appellate court upholds the judgment of the district court, the execution of the judgment shall proceed. The clerk of court shall not disperse any rent in arrears paid by the defendant appellant until all appeals have been resolved.

§ 42-35. Restitution of tenant, if case quashed, etc., on appeal. If the proceedings before the magistrate are brought before a district court and quashed, or judgment is given against the plaintiff, the district or other court in which final judgment is given shall, if necessary, restore the defendant to the possession, and issue such writs as are proper for that purpose.

§ 42-36. Damages to tenant for dispossession, if proceedings quashed, etc. If, by order of the magistrate, the plaintiff is put in possession, and the proceedings shall afterwards be quashed or reversed, the defendant may recover damages of the plaintiff for his removal.

§ 42-36.1. Lease or rental of manufactured homes. The provisions of this Article shall apply to the lease or rental of manufactured homes, as defined in G.S. 143-145.

§ 42-36.1A. Judgments for possession more than 30 days old. Prior to obtaining execution of a judgment that has been entered for more than 30 days for possession of demised premises, a landlord shall sign an affidavit stating that the landlord has neither entered into a formal lease with the defendant nor accepted rental money from the defendant for any period of time after entry of the judgment.

§ 42-36.2. Notice to tenant of execution of writ for possession of property; storage of evicted tenant's personal property.

(a) When Sheriff May Remove Property. -- Before removing a tenant's personal property from demised premises pursuant to a writ for possession of real property or an order, the sheriff shall give the tenant notice of the approximate time the writ will be executed. The time within which the sheriff shall have to execute the writ shall be no more than seven days from the sheriff's receipt thereof. The sheriff shall remove the tenant's property, as provided in the writ, no earlier than the time specified in the notice, unless:

(1) The landlord, or his authorized agent, signs a statement saying that the tenant's property can remain on the premises, in which case the sheriff shall simply lock the premises; or

(2) The landlord, or his authorized agent, signs a statement saying that the landlord does not want to eject the tenant because the tenant has paid all court costs charged to him and has satisfied his indebtedness to the landlord.

Upon receipt of either statement by the landlord, the sheriff shall return the writ unexecuted to the issuing clerk of court and shall make a notation on the writ of his reasons. The sheriff shall attach a copy of the landlord's statement to the writ. If the writ is returned unexecuted because the landlord signed a statement described in subdivision (2) of this subsection, the clerk shall make an entry of satisfaction on the judgment docket. If the sheriff padlocks, the costs of the proceeding shall be charged as part of the court costs.

(b) Sheriff May Store Property. — When the sheriff removes the personal property of an evicted tenant from demised premises pursuant to a writ or order the tenant shall take possession of his property. If the tenant fails or refuses to take possession of his property, the sheriff may deliver the property to any storage warehouse in the county, or in an adjoining county if no storage warehouse is located in that county, for storage. The sheriff may require the landlord to advance the cost of delivering the property to a storage warehouse plus the cost of one month's storage before delivering the property to a storage warehouse. If a landlord refuses to advance these costs when requested to do so by the sheriff, the sheriff shall not remove the tenant's property, but shall return the writ unexecuted to the issuing clerk of court with a notation thereon of his reason for not executing the writ. Within 10 days of the landlord's being placed in lawful possession by execution of a writ of possession and upon the tenant's request within that 10-day period, the landlord shall release possession of the property to the tenant during regular business hours or at a time agreed upon. During the 10-day period after being placed in lawful possession by execution of a writ of possession, a landlord may move for storage purposes, but shall not throw away, dispose of, or sell any items of personal property remaining on the premises unless otherwise provided for in this Chapter. After the expiration of the 10-day period, the landlord may throw away, dispose of, or sell the property in accordance with the provisions of G.S. 42-25.9(g). If the tenant does not request release of the property within 10 days, all costs of summary ejectment, execution and storage proceedings shall be charged to the tenant as court costs and shall constitute a lien against the stored property or a claim against any remaining balance of the proceeds of a warehouseman's lien sale.

(c) Liability of the Sheriff. — A sheriff who stores a tenant's property pursuant to this section and any person acting under the sheriff's direction, control, or employment shall be liable for any claims arising out of the willful or wanton negligence in storing the tenant's property.

(d) Notice. — The notice required by subsection (a) shall inform the tenant that failure to request possession of any property on the premises within 10 days of execution may result in the property being thrown away, disposed of, or sold. Notice shall be made by one of the following methods:

(1) By delivering a copy of the notice to the tenant or his authorized agent at least two days before the time stated in the notice for serving the writ;

(2) By leaving a copy of the notice at the tenant's dwelling or usual place of abode with a person of suitable age and discretion who resides there at least two days before the time stated in the notice for serving the writ; or

(3) By mailing a copy of the notice by first-class mail to the tenant at his last known address at least five days before the time stated in the notice for serving the writ.

ARTICLE 4A.

Retaliatory Eviction.

§ 42-37.1. Defense of retaliatory eviction.

(a) It is the public policy of the State of North Carolina to protect tenants and other persons whose residence in the household is explicitly or implicitly known to the landlord, who seek to exercise their rights to decent, safe, and sanitary housing. Therefore, the following activities of such persons are protected by law:

(1) A good faith complaint or request for repairs to the landlord, his employee, or his agent about conditions or defects in the premises that the landlord is obligated to repair under G.S. 42-42;

(2) A good faith complaint to a government agency about a landlord's alleged violation of any health or safety law, or any regulation, code, ordinance, or State or federal law that regulates premises used for dwelling purposes;

(3) A government authority's issuance of a formal complaint to a landlord concerning premises rented by a tenant;

(4) A good faith attempt to exercise, secure or enforce any rights existing under a valid lease or rental agreement or under State or federal law; or

(5) A good faith attempt to organize, join, or become otherwise involved with, any organization promoting or enforcing tenants' rights.

(b) In an action for summary ejectment pursuant to G.S. 42-26, a tenant may raise the affirmative defense of retaliatory eviction and may present evidence that the landlord's action is substantially in response to the occurrence within 12 months of the filing of such action of one or more of the protected acts described in subsection (a) of this section.

(c) Notwithstanding subsections (a) and (b) of this section, a landlord may prevail in an action for summary ejectment if:

(1) The tenant breached the covenant to pay rent or any other substantial covenant of the lease for which the tenant may be evicted, and such breach is the reason for the eviction; or

(2) In a case of a tenancy for a definite period of time where the tenant has no option to renew the lease, the tenant holds over after expiration of the term; or

(3) The violation of G.S. 42-42 complained of was caused primarily by the willful or negligent conduct of the tenant, member of the tenant's household, or their guests or invitees; or

(4) Compliance with the applicable building or housing code requires demolition or major alteration or remodeling that cannot be accomplished without completely displacing the tenant's household; or

(5) The landlord seeks to recover possession on the basis of a good faith notice to quit the premises, which notice was delivered prior to the occurrence of any of the activities protected by subsections (a) and (b) of this section; or

(6) The landlord seeks in good faith to recover possession at the end of the tenant's term for use as the landlord's own abode, to demolish or make major alterations or remodeling of the dwelling unit in a manner that requires the complete displacement of the tenant's household, or to terminate for at least six months the use of the property as a rental dwelling unit.

§ 42-37.2. Remedies.

(a) If the court finds that an ejectment action is retaliatory, as defined by this Article, it shall deny the request for ejectment; provided, that a dismissal of the request for ejectment shall not prevent the landlord from receiving payments for rent due or any other appropriate judgment.

(b) The rights and remedies created by this Article are supplementary to all existing common law and statutory rights and remedies.

§ 42-37.3. Waiver. Any waiver by a tenant or a member of his household of the rights and remedies created by this Article is void as contrary to public policy.

ARTICLE 5.

Residential Rental Agreements.

§ 42-38. Application. This Article determines the rights, obligations, and remedies under a rental agreement for a dwelling unit within this State.

§ 42-39. Exclusions.

(a) The provisions of this Article shall not apply to transient occupancy in a hotel, motel, or similar lodging subject to regulation by the Commission for Health Services.

(b) Nothing in this Article shall apply to any dwelling furnished without charge or rent.

§ **42-40. Definitions.** For the purpose of this Article, the following definitions shall apply:

(1) "Action" includes recoupment, counterclaim, defense, setoff, and any other proceeding including an action for possession.

(2) "Premises" means a dwelling unit, including mobile homes or mobile home spaces, and the structure of which it is a part and facilities and appurtenances therein and grounds, areas, and facilities normally held out for the use of residential tenants who are using the dwelling unit as their primary residence.

(3) "Landlord" means any owner and any rental management company, rental agency, or any other person having the actual or apparent authority of an agent to perform the duties imposed by this Article.

§ **42-41. Mutuality of obligations.** The tenant's obligation to pay rent under the rental agreement or assignment and to comply with G.S. 42-43 and the landlord's obligation to comply with G.S. 42-42(a) shall be mutually dependent.

§ 42-42. Landlord to provide fit premises.

(a) The landlord shall:

(1) Comply with the current applicable building and housing codes, whether enacted before or after October 1, 1977, to the extent required by the operation of such codes; no new requirement is imposed by this subdivision (a)(1) if a structure is exempt from a current building code.

(2) Make all repairs and do whatever is necessary to put and keep the premises in a fit and habitable condition.

(3) Keep all common areas of the premises in safe condition.

(4) Maintain in good and safe working order and promptly repair all electrical, plumbing, sanitary, heating, ventilating, air conditioning, and other facilities and appliances supplied or required to be supplied by the landlord provided that notification of needed repairs is made to the landlord in writing by the tenant, except in emergency situations.

(5) Provide operable smoke detectors, either battery-operated or electrical, having an Underwriters' Laboratories, Inc., listing or other equivalent national testing laboratory approval, and install the smoke detectors in accordance with either the standards of the National Fire Protection Association or the minimum protection designated in the manufacturer's instructions, which the landlord shall retain or provide as proof of compliance. The landlord shall replace or repair the smoke detectors within 15 days of receipt of notification if the landlord is notified of needed replacement or repairs in writing by the tenant. The landlord shall ensure that a smoke detector is operable and in good repair at the beginning of each tenancy. Unless the landlord and the tenant have a written agreement to the contrary, the landlord shall place new batteries in a battery-operated smoke detector at the beginning of a tenancy and the tenant shall replace the batteries as needed during the tenancy. Failure of the tenant to replace the batteries as needed shall not be considered as negligence on the part of the tenant or the landlord.

(b) The landlord is not released of his obligations under any part of this section by the tenant's explicit or implicit acceptance of the landlord's failure to provide premises complying with this section, whether done before the lease was made, when it was made, or after it was made, unless a governmental subdivision imposes an impediment to repair for a specific period of time not to exceed six months. Notwithstanding the provisions of this subsection, the landlord and tenant are not prohibited from making a subsequent written contract wherein the tenant agrees to perform specified work on the premises, provided that said contract is supported by adequate consideration other than the letting of the premises and is not made with the purpose or effect of evading the landlord's obligations under this Article.

§ 42-43. Tenant to maintain dwelling unit.

(a) The tenant shall:

(1) Keep that part of the premises that the tenant occupies and uses as clean and safe as the conditions of the premises permit and cause no unsafe or unsanitary conditions in the common areas and remainder of the premises that the tenant uses.

(2) Dispose of all ashes, rubbish, garbage, and other waste in a clean and safe manner.

(3) Keep all plumbing fixtures in the dwelling unit or used by the tenant as clean as their condition permits.

(4) Not deliberately or negligently destroy, deface, damage, or remove any part of the premises, nor render inoperable the smoke detector provided by the landlord, or knowingly permit any person to do so.

(5) Comply with any and all obligations imposed upon the tenant by current applicable building and housing codes.

(6) Be responsible for all damage, defacement, or removal of any property inside a dwelling unit in the tenant's exclusive control unless the damage, defacement or removal was due to ordinary wear and tear, acts of the landlord or the landlord's agent, defective products supplied or repairs

authorized by the landlord, acts of third parties not invitees of the tenant, or natural forces.

(7) Notify the landlord, in writing, of the need for replacement of or repairs to a smoke detector. The landlord shall ensure that a smoke detector is operable and in good repair at the beginning of each tenancy. Unless the landlord and the tenant have a written agreement to the contrary, the landlord shall place new batteries in a battery-operated smoke detector at the beginning of a tenancy and the tenant shall replace the batteries as needed during the tenancy. Failure of the tenant to replace the batteries as needed shall not be considered as negligence on the part of the tenant or the landlord.

(b) The landlord shall notify the tenant in writing of any breaches of the tenant's obligations under this section except in emergency situations.

§ 42-44. General remedies, penalties, and limitations.

(a) Any right or obligation declared by this Chapter is enforceable by civil action, in addition to other remedies of law and in equity.

(a1) If a landlord fails to provide, install, replace, or repair a smoke detector under the provisions of G.S. 42-42(a)(5) within 30 days of having received written notice from the tenant or any agent of State or local government of the landlord's failure to do so, the landlord shall be responsible for an infraction and shall be subject to a fine of not more than two hundred fifty dollars ($250.00) for each violation. The landlord may temporarily disconnect a smoke detector in a dwelling unit or common area for construction or rehabilitation activities when such activities are likely to activate the smoke detector or make it inactive.

(a2) If a smoke detector is disabled or damaged, other than through actions of the landlord, the landlord's agents, or acts of God, the tenant shall reimburse the landlord the reasonable and actual cost for repairing or replacing the smoke detector within 30 days of having received written notice from the landlord or any agent of State or local government of the need for the tenant to make such reimbursement. If the tenant fails to make reimbursement within 30 days, the tenant shall be responsible for an infraction and subject to a fine of not more than one hundred dollars ($100.00) for each violation. The tenant may temporarily disconnect a smoke detector in a dwelling unit to replace the batteries or when it has been inadvertently activated.

(b) Repealed.

(c) The tenant may not unilaterally withhold rent prior to a judicial determination of a right to do so.

(d) A violation of this Article shall not constitute negligence per se.

§ 42-45. Early termination of rental agreement by military personnel.

(a) Any member of the United States Armed Forces who (i) is required to move pursuant to permanent change of station orders to depart 50 miles or more from the location of the dwelling unit, or (ii) is prematurely or involuntarily discharged or released from active duty with the United States Armed Forces, may terminate his rental agreement for a dwelling unit by providing the landlord with a written notice of termination to be effective on a date stated in the notice that is at least 30 days after the landlord's receipt of the notice. The notice to the landlord must be accompanied by either a copy of the official military orders or a written verification signed by the member's commanding officer.

Upon termination of a rental agreement under this section, the tenant is liable for the rent due under the rental agreement prorated to the effective date of the termination payable at such time as would have otherwise been required by the terms of the rental agreement. The tenant is not liable for any other rent or damages due to the early termination of the tenancy except the liquidated damages provided in subsection (b) of this section. If a member terminates the rental agreement pursuant to this section 14 or more days prior to occupancy, no damages or penalties of any kind shall be due.

(b) In consideration of early termination of the rental agreement, the tenant is liable to the landlord for liquidated damages provided the tenant has completed less than nine months of the tenancy and the landlord has suffered actual damages due to loss of the tenancy. The liquidated damages shall be in an amount no greater than one month's rent if the tenant has completed less than six months of the tenancy as of the effective date of termination, or one-half of one month's rent if the tenant has completed at least six but less than nine months of the tenancy as of the effective date of termination.

(c) The provisions of this section may not be waived or modified by the agreement of the parties under any circumstances. Nothing in this section shall affect the rights established by G.S. 42-3.

§ 42-46. Late fees.

(a) In all residential rental agreements in which a definite time for the payment of the rent is fixed, the parties may agree to a late fee not to exceed fifteen dollars ($15.00) or five percent (5%) of the rental payment, whichever is greater, to be charged by the lessor if any rental payment is five days or more late.

(b) A late fee under this section may be imposed only one time for each late rental payment. A late fee for a specific late rental payment may not be deducted from a subsequent rental payment so as to cause the subsequent rental payment to be in default.

(c) Any provision of a residential rental agreement contrary to the provisions of this section is against the public policy of this State and therefore void and unenforceable.

ARTICLE 6.

Tenant Security Deposit Act.

§ 42-50. Deposits from the tenant. Security deposits from the tenant in residential dwelling units shall be deposited in a trust account with a licensed and insured bank or savings institution located in the State of North Carolina or the landlord may, at his option, furnish a bond from an insurance company licensed to do business in North Carolina. The security deposits from the tenant may be held in a trust account outside of the State of North Carolina only if the landlord provides the tenant with an adequate bond in the amount of said deposits. The landlord or his agent shall notify the tenant within 30 days after the beginning of the lease term of the name and address of the bank or institution where his deposit is currently located or the name of the insurance company providing the bond.

§ 42-51. Permitted uses of the deposit. Security deposits for residential dwelling units shall be permitted only for the tenant's possible nonpayment of rent, damage to the premises, nonfulfillment of rental period, any unpaid bills which become a lien against the demised property due to the tenant's occupancy, costs of re-renting the premises after breach by the tenant, costs of removal and storage of tenant's property after a summary ejectment proceeding or court costs in connection with terminating a tenancy. Such security deposit shall not exceed an amount equal to two weeks' rent if a tenancy is week to week, one and one-half months' rent if a tenancy is month to month, and two months' rent for terms greater than month to month. These deposits must be fully accounted for by the landlord as set forth in G.S. 42-52.

§ 42-52. Landlord's obligations. Upon termination of the tenancy, money held by the landlord as security may be applied as permitted in G.S. 42-51 or, if not so applied, shall be refunded to the tenant. In either case the landlord in writing shall itemize any damage and mail or deliver same to the tenant, together with the balance of the security deposit, no later than 30 days after termination of the tenancy and delivery of possession by the tenant. If the tenant's address is unknown the landlord shall apply the deposit as permitted in G.S. 42-51 after a period of 30 days and the landlord shall hold the balance of the deposit for collection by the tenant for at least six months. The landlord may not withhold as damages part of the security deposit for conditions that are due to normal wear and tear nor may the landlord retain an amount from the security deposit which exceeds his actual damages.

§ 42-53. Pet deposits. Notwithstanding the provisions of this section, the landlord may charge a reasonable, nonrefundable fee for pets kept by the tenant on the premises.

§ 42-54. Transfer of dwelling units. Upon termination of the landlord's interest in the dwelling unit in question, whether by sale, assignment, death, appointment of receiver or otherwise, the landlord or his agent shall, within 30 days, do one of the following acts, either of which shall relieve him of further liability with respect to such payment or deposit:

(1) Transfer the portion of such payment or deposit remaining after any lawful deductions made under this section to the landlord's successor in interest and thereafter notify the tenant by mail of such transfer and of the transferee's name and address; or

(2) Return the portion of such payment or deposit remaining after any lawful deductions made under this section to the tenant.

§ 42-55. Remedies. If the landlord or the landlord's successor in interest fails to account for and refund the balance of the tenant's security deposit as required by this Article, the tenant may institute a civil action to require the accounting of and the recovery of the balance of the deposit. In addition to other remedies at law and equity, the tenant may recover damages resulting from noncompliance by the landlord; and upon a finding by the court that the party against whom judgment is rendered was in willful noncompliance with this Article, the court may, in its discretion, allow a reasonable attorney's fee to the duly licensed attorney representing the prevailing party, such attorney's fee to be taxed as part of the cost of court.

§ 42-56. Application of Article. The provisions of this Article shall apply to all persons, firms, or corporations engaged in the business of renting or managing residential dwelling units, excluding single rooms, on a weekly, monthly or annual basis.

ARTICLE 7.

Expedited Eviction of Drug Traffickers and Other Criminals.

§ 42-59. Definitions. As used in this Article:

(1) "Complete eviction" means the eviction and removal of a tenant and all members of the tenant's household.

(2) "Criminal activity" means (i) activity that would constitute a violation of G.S. 90-95 other than a violation of G.S. 90-95(a)(3), or a conspiracy to violate any provision of G.S. 90-95 other than G.S. 90-95(a)(3); or (ii) other criminal activity that threatens the health, safety, or right of peaceful enjoyment of the entire premises by other residents or employees of the landlord.

(3) "Entire premises" or "leased residential premises" means a house, building, mobile home, or apartment, whether publicly or privately owned, which is leased for residential purposes. These terms include the entire building or complex of buildings or mobile home park and all real property of any nature appurtenant thereto and used in connection therewith, including all individual rental units, streets, sidewalks, and common areas. These terms do not include a hotel, motel, or other guest house or part thereof rented to a transient guest.

(4) "Felony" means a criminal offense that constitutes a felony under North Carolina law.

(5) "Guest" means any natural person who has been given express or implied permission by a tenant, a member of the tenant's household, or another guest of the tenant to enter an individual rental unit or any portion of the entire premises.

(6) "Individual rental unit" means an apartment or individual dwelling or accommodation which is leased to a particular tenant, whether or not it is used or occupied or intended to be used or occupied by a single family or household.

(7) "Landlord" means a person, entity, corporation, or governmental authority or agency who or which owns, operates, or manages any leased residential premises.

(8) "Partial eviction" means the eviction and removal of specified persons from a leased residential premises.

(9) "Resident" means any natural person who lawfully resides in a leased residential premises who is not a signatory to a lease or otherwise has no contractual relationship to a landlord. The term includes members of the household of a tenant.

(10) "Tenant" means any natural person or entity who is a named party or signatory to a lease or rental agreement, and who occupies, resides in, or has a legal right to possess and use an individual rental unit.

§ 42-59.1. Statement of Public Policy. The General Assembly recognizes that the residents of this State have the right to the peaceful, safe, and quiet enjoyment of their homes. The General Assembly further recognizes that these rights, as well as the health, safety, and welfare of residents, are often jeopardized by the criminal activity of other residents of rented residential property, but that landlords are often unable to remove those residents engaged in criminal activity. In order to ensure that residents of this State can have the peaceful, safe, and quiet enjoyment of their homes, the provisions of this Article are deemed to apply to all residential rental agreements in this State.

§ 42-60. Nature of actions and jurisdiction. The causes of action established in this Article are civil actions to remove tenants or other persons from leased residential premises. These actions shall be brought in the district court of the county where the individual rental unit is located. If the plaintiff files the complaint as a small claim, the parties shall not be entitled to discovery from the magistrate. However, if such a case is filed originally in the district court or is appealed from the judgment of a magistrate for a new trial in the district court, all of the procedures and remedies in this Article shall be applicable.

§ 42-61. Standard of proof. The civil causes of action established in this Article shall be proved by a preponderance of the evidence, except as otherwise expressly provided in G.S. 42-64.

§ 42-62. Parties.

(a) Who May Bring Action. -- A civil action pursuant to this Article may be brought by the landlord of a leased residential premises, or the landlord's agent, as provided for in G.S. 1-57 of the General Statutes and in Article 3 of this Chapter.

(b) Defendants to the Action. -- A civil action pursuant to this Article may be brought against any person within the jurisdiction of the court, including a tenant, adult or minor member of the tenant's household, guest, or resident of the leased residential premises. If any defendant's true name is unknown to the plaintiff, process may issue against the defendant under a fictitious name, stating it to be fictitious and adding an appropriate description sufficient to identify him or her.

(c) Notice to Defendants. — A complaint initiating an action pursuant to this Article shall be served in the same manner as serving complaints in civil actions pursuant to G.S. 1A- 1, Rule 4 and G.S. 42-29.

§ 42-63. Remedies and judicial orders.

(a) Grounds for Complete Eviction. — Subject to the provisions of G.S. 42-64 and pursuant to G.S 42-68, the court shall order the immediate eviction of a tenant and all other residents of the tenant's individual unit where it finds that:

(1) Criminal activity has occurred on or within the individual rental unit leased to the tenant; or
(2) The individual rental unit leased to the tenant was used in any way in furtherance of or to promote criminal activity; or
(3) The tenant, any member of the tenant's household, or any guest has engaged in criminal activity on or in the immediate vicinity of any portion of the entire premises; or
(4) The tenant has given permission to or invited a person to return or reenter any portion of the entire premises, knowing that the person has been removed and barred from the entire premises pursuant to this Article or the reasonable rules and regulations of a publicly assisted landlord; or

(5) The tenant has failed to notify law enforcement or the landlord immediately upon learning that a person who has been removed and barred from the tenant's individual rental unit pursuant to this Article has returned to or reentered the tenant's individual rental unit.

(b) Grounds for Partial Eviction and Issuance of Removal Orders. — The court shall, subject to the provisions of G.S. 42- 64, order the immediate removal from the entire premises of any person other than the tenant, including an adult or minor member of the tenant's household, where the court finds that such person has engaged in criminal activity on or in the immediate vicinity of any portion of the leased residential premises. Persons removed pursuant to this section shall be barred from returning to or reentering any portion of the entire premises.

(c) Conditional Eviction Orders Directed Against the Tenant. — Where the court finds that a member of the tenant's household or a guest of the tenant has engaged in criminal activity on or in the immediate vicinity of any portion of the leased residential premises, but such person has not been named as a party defendant, has not appeared in the action or otherwise has not been subjected to the jurisdiction of the court, a conditional eviction order issued pursuant to subsection (b) of this section shall be directed against the tenant, and shall provide that as an express condition of the tenancy, the tenant shall not give permission to or invite the barred person or persons to return to or reenter any portion of the entire premises. The tenant shall acknowledge in writing that the tenant understands the terms of the court's order, and that the tenant further understands that the failure to comply with the court's order will result in the mandatory termination of the tenancy pursuant to G.S. 42-68.

§ 42-64. Affirmative defense or exemption to a complete eviction.

(a) Affirmative Defense. — The court shall refrain from ordering the complete eviction of a tenant pursuant to G.S. 42- 63(a) where the tenant has established that the tenant was not involved in the criminal activity and that:

(1) The tenant did not know or have reason to know that criminal activity was occurring or would likely occur on or within the individual rental unit, that the individual rental unit was used in any way in furtherance of or to promote criminal activity, or that any member of the tenant's household or any guest has engaged in criminal activity on or in the immediate vicinity of any portion of the entire premises; or

(2) The tenant had done everything that could reasonably be expected under the circumstances to prevent the commission of the criminal activity, such as requesting the landlord to remove the offending household member's name from the lease, reporting prior criminal activity to appropriate law enforcement authorities, seeking assistance from social service or counseling agencies, denying permission, if feasible, for the offending household member to reside in the unit, or seeking assistance from church or religious organizations.

Notwithstanding the court's denial of eviction of the tenant, if the plaintiff has proven that an evictable offense under G.S. 42-63 was committed by someone other than the tenant, the court shall order such other relief as the court deems appropriate to protect the interests of the landlord and neighbors of the tenant, including the partial eviction of the culpable household members pursuant to G.S. 42-63(b) and conditional eviction orders under G.S. 42-63(c).

(b) Subsequent Affirmative Defense to a Complete Eviction. — The affirmative defense set forth in subsection (a) of this section shall not be available to a tenant in a subsequent action brought pursuant to this Article unless the tenant can establish by clear and convincing evidence that no reasonable person could have foreseen the occurrence of the subsequent criminal activity or that the tenant had done everything reasonably expected under the circumstances to prevent the commission of the second criminal activity.

(c) Exemption. — Where the grounds for a complete eviction have been established, the court shall order the eviction of the tenant unless, taking into account the circumstances of the criminal activity and the condition of the tenant, the court is clearly convinced that immediate eviction or removal would be a serious injustice, the prevention of which overrides the need to protect the rights, safety, and health of the other tenants and residents of the leased residential premises. The burden of proof for the exemption set forth shall be by clear and convincing evidence.

§ 42-65. Obstructing the execution or enforcement of a removal or eviction order. Any person who knowingly violates any order issued pursuant to this Article or who knowingly interferes with, obstructs, impairs, or prevents any law enforcement officer from enforcing or executing any order issued pursuant to this Article, shall be subject to criminal contempt under Article 1 of Chapter 5A of the General Statutes. Nothing in this section shall be construed in any way to preclude or preempt prosecution for any other criminal offense.

§ 42-66. Motion to enforce eviction and removal orders.

(a) A motion to enforce an eviction or removal order issued pursuant to G.S. 42-63(b) or (c) shall be heard on an expedited basis and within 15 days of the service of the motion.

(b) Mandatory Eviction. — The court shall order the immediate eviction of the tenant where it finds that:

(1) The tenant has given permission to or invited any person removed or barred from the leased residential premises pursuant to this Article to return to or reenter any portion of the premises; or

(2) The tenant has failed to notify appropriate law enforcement authorities or the landlord immediately upon learning that any person who had been removed and barred pursuant to this Article has returned to or reentered the tenant's individual rental unit; or

(3) The tenant has otherwise knowingly violated an express term or condition of any order issued by court pursuant to this Article.

§ 42-67. **Impermissible defense.** It shall not be a defense to an action brought pursuant to this Article that the criminal activity was an isolated incident or otherwise has not recurred. Nor is it a defense that the person who actually engaged in the criminal activity no longer resides in the tenant's individual rental unit. However, evidence of such facts may be admissible if offered to support affirmative defenses or grounds for an exemption pursuant to G.S. 42-64.

§ 42-68. **Expedited proceedings.** Where the complaint is filed as a small claim, the expedited process for summary ejectment, as provided in Article 3 of this Chapter and Chapter 7A of the General Statutes, applies. Where the complaint is filed initially in the district court or a judgment by the magistrate is appealed to the district court, the procedure in G.S. 42-34(b) through (g), if applicable, and the following procedures apply:

(1) Expedited Hearing. — When a complaint is filed initiating an action pursuant to this Article, the court shall set the matter for a hearing which shall be held on an expedited basis and within the first term of court falling after 30 days from the service of the complaint on all defendants or from service of notice of appeal from a magistrate's judgment, unless either party obtains a continuance. However, where a defendant files a counterclaim, the court shall reset the trial for the first term of court falling after 30 days from the defendant's service of the counterclaim.

(2) Standards for Continuances. — The court shall not grant a continuance, nor shall it stay the civil proceedings pending the disposition of any related criminal proceedings, except as required to complete permitted discovery, to have the plaintiff reply to a counterclaim, or for compelling and extraordinary reasons or on application of the district attorney for good cause shown.

(3) When Presented. — The defendant in an action brought in district court pursuant to this Article shall serve an answer within 20 days after service of the summons and complaint, or within 20 days after service of the appeal to district court when the action was initially brought in small claims court. The plaintiff shall serve a reply to a counterclaim in the answer within 20 days after service of the answer.

(4) Extensions of Time for Filing. — The parties to an action brought pursuant to this Article shall not be entitled to an extension of time for completing an act required by subdivision (3) of this section, except for compelling and extraordinary reasons.

(5) Default. — A party to an action brought pursuant to this Article who fails to plead in accordance with the time periods in subdivision (3) of this ection shall be subject to the provisions of G.S. 1A-1, Rule 55.

(6) Rules of Civil Procedure. — Unless otherwise provided for in this Article, G.S. 1A-1, the Rules of Civil Procedure, shall apply in the district court to all actions brought pursuant to this Article.

§ 42-69. **Relation to criminal proceedings.**

(a) Criminal Proceedings, Conviction, or Adjudication Not Required. — The fact that a criminal prosecution involving the criminal activity is not commenced or, if commenced, has not yet been concluded or has terminated without a conviction or adjudication of delinquency shall not preclude a civil action or the issuance of any order pursuant to this Article.

(b) Effect of Conviction or Adjudication. -- Where a criminal prosecution involving the criminal activity results in a final criminal conviction or adjudication of delinquency, such adjudication or conviction shall be considered in the civil action as conclusive proof that the criminal activity occurred.

(c) Admissibility of Criminal Trial Recordings or Transcripts. — Any evidence or testimony admitted in the criminal proceeding, including recordings or transcripts of the adult or juvenile criminal proceedings, whether or not they have been transcribed, may be admitted in the civil action initiated pursuant to this Article.

(d) Use of Sealed Criminal Proceeding Records. — In the event that the evidence or records of a criminal proceeding which did not result in a conviction or adjudication of delinquency have been sealed by court order, the court in a civil action brought pursuant to this Article may order such evidence or records, whether or not they have been transcribed, to be unsealed if the court finds that such evidence or records would be relevant to the fair disposition of the civil action.

§ 42-70. **Discovery.**

(a) The parties to an action brought pursuant to this Article shall be entitled to conduct discovery, if the action is filed originally in or appealed to the district court, only in accordance with this section.

(b) Any defendant must initiate all discovery within the time allowed by this Article for the filing of an answer or counterclaim.

(c) The plaintiff must initiate all discovery within 20 days of service of an answer or counterclaim by a defendant.

(d) All parties served with interrogatories, requests for production of documents, and requests for admissions under G.S. 1A-1, Rules 33, 34, and 36 shall serve their responses within 20 days.

(e) Upon application by the plaintiff, or agreement of the parties, the court shall issue a preliminary injunction against all alleged illegal activity by the defendant or other identified parties who are residents of the individual rental unit or guests of defendants, pending the completion of discovery and any other wait before the trial has occurred.

§ 42-71. **Protection of threatened witnesses or affiants.** If proof necessary to establish the grounds for eviction depends, in whole or in part, upon the affidavits or testimony of witnesses who are not peace officers, the court may, upon a showing of prior threats of violence or acts of violence by any defendant or any other person, issue orders to protect those witnesses, including the nondisclosure of the name, address, or any other information which may identify those witnesses.

§ 42-72. **Availability of law enforcement resources to plaintiffs or potential plaintiffs.** A law enforcement agency may make available to any person or entity authorized to bring an action pursuant to this Article any police report or edited portion thereof, or forensic laboratory report or edited portion thereof, concerning criminal activity committed on or in the immediate vicinity of the leased residential premises. A law enforcement agency may also make any officer or officers available to testify as a fact witness or expert witness in a civil action brought pursuant to this Article. The agency shall not disclose such information where, in the agency's opinion, such disclosure would jeopardize an investigation, prosecution, or other proceeding, or where such disclosure would violate any federal or State statute.

§ 42-73. **Collection of rent.** A landlord shall be entitled to collect rent due and owing with knowledge of any illegal acts that violate the provisions of this act without such collection constituting a waiver of the alleged defaults.

§ 42-74. **Preliminary or emergency relief.** The district court shall have the authority at any time to issue a temporary restraining order, grant a preliminary injunction, or take such other actions as the court deems necessary to enjoin or prevent the commission of criminal activity on or in the immediate vicinity of leased residential premises, or otherwise to protect the rights and interests of all tenants and residents. A violation of any such duly issued order or preliminary relief shall subject the violator to civil or criminal contempt.

§ 42-75. **Cumulative remedies.** The causes of action and remedies authorized by this Article shall be cumulative with each other and shall be in addition to, not in lieu of, any other causes of action or remedies which may be available at law or equity, including causes of action and remedies based on express provisions of the lease not contrary to this Article.

§ 42-76. **Civil immunity.** Any person or organization who, in good faith, institutes, participates in, or encourages a person or entity to institute or participate in a civil action brought pursuant to this Article, or who in good faith provides any information relied upon by any person or entity in instituting or participating in a civil action pursuant to this Article shall have immunity from any civil liability that might otherwise be incurred or imposed. Any such person or organization shall have the same immunity from civil liability with respect to testimony given in any judicial proceeding conducted pursuant to this Article.

Appendix B
Eviction Flowcharts and Legal Holidays

On the next two pages are flowcharts which show each step in the eviction process. The first is for an eviction for nonpayment of rent. The second is for an eviction based on the tenant's breach of some clause of the lease other than payment of rent, or for the tenant's violation of some aspect of the Landlord Tenant Act.

On the final page of this appendix is a list of the legal holidays in North Carolina.

Eviction Flow Chart–Non-Payment of Rent

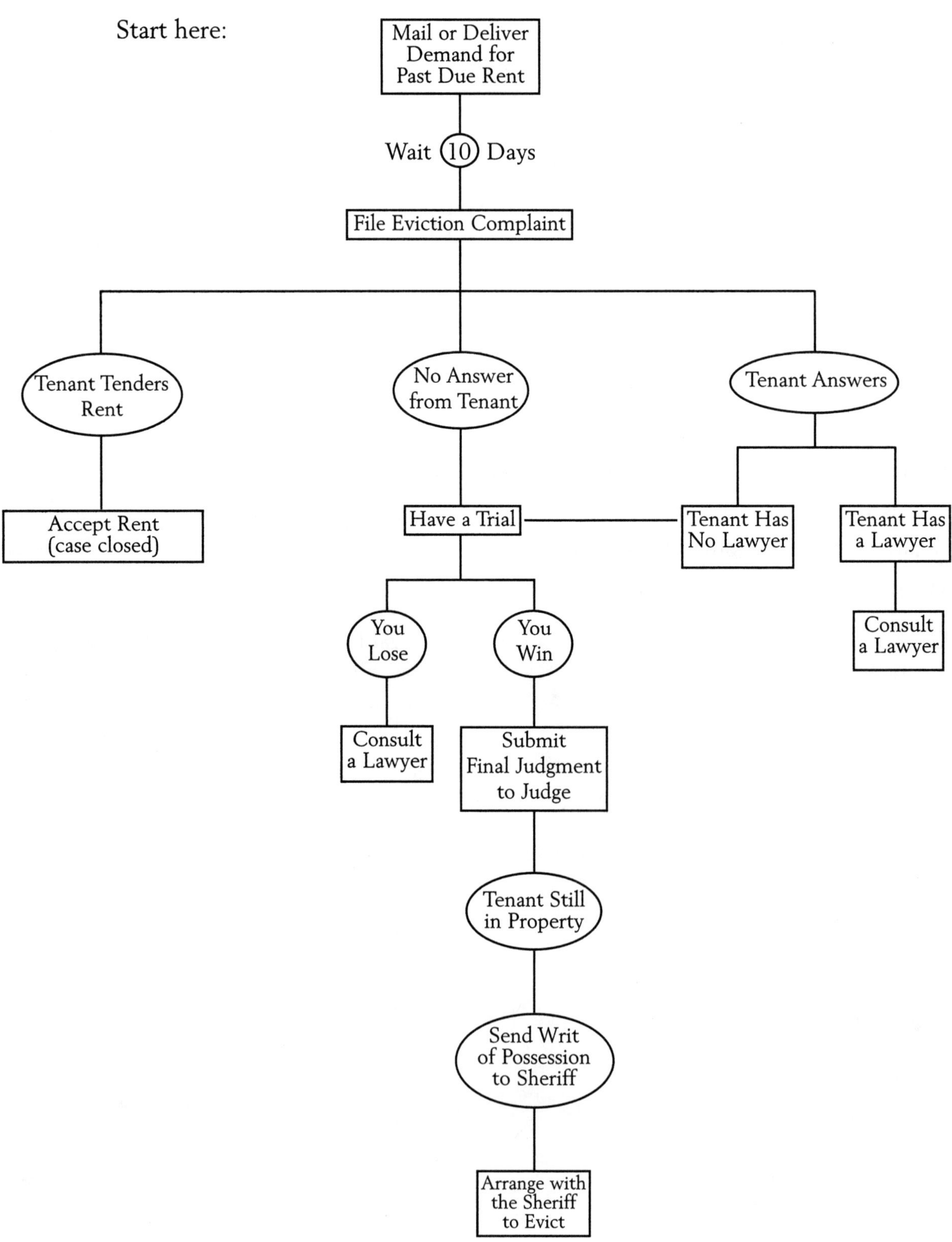

Eviction Flow Chart
Breach of Lease or Expiration of Terms

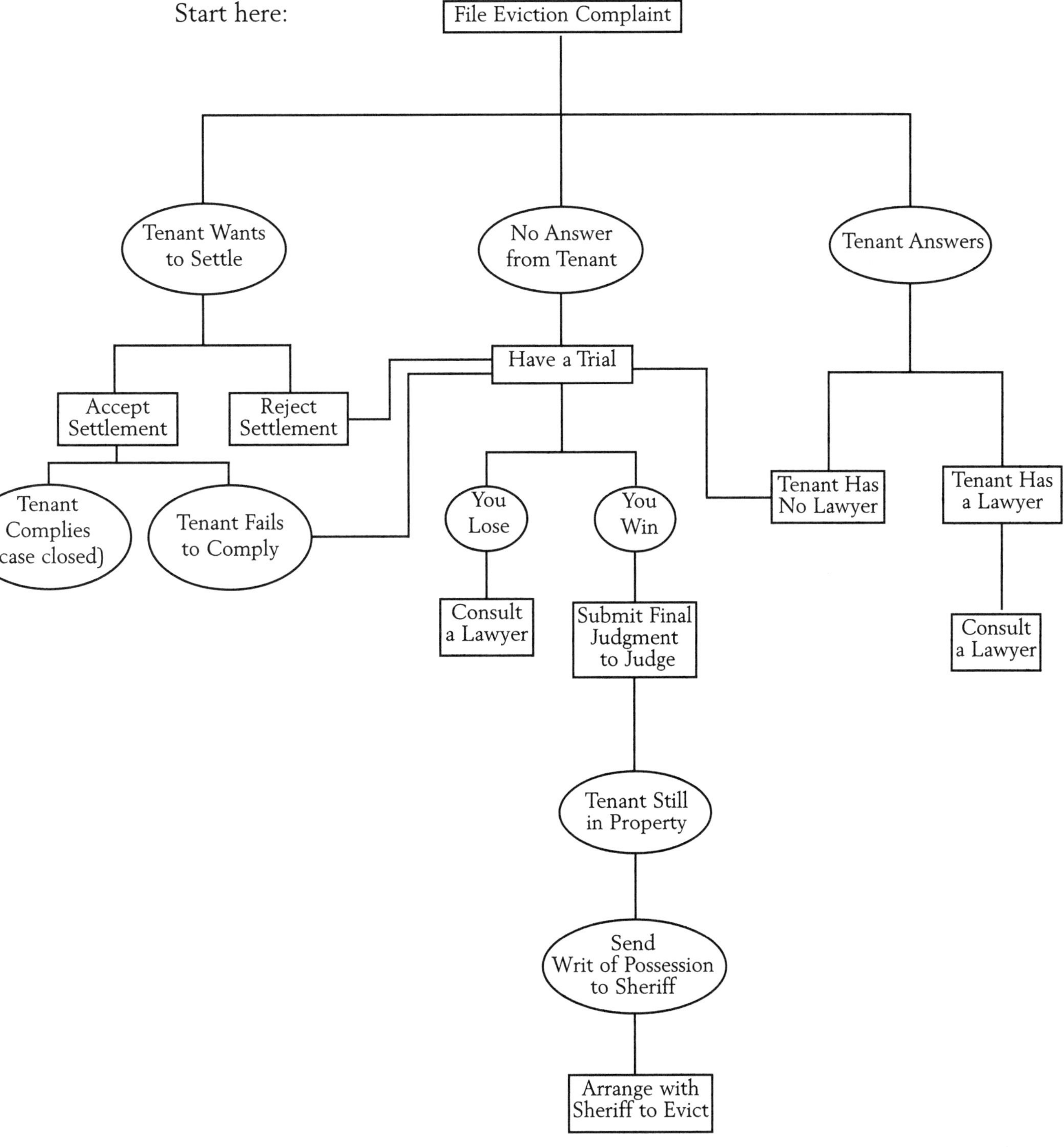

Legal Holidays in North Carolina
(North Carolina General Statutes, Chapter 103)

New Year's Day	January 1
Dr. Martin Luther King, Jr. Day	Third Monday in January
Robert E. Lee's Birthday	Jan. 19
Greek Independence Day	March 25
George Washington's Birthday	Third Monday in February
Good Friday	(varies)
Anniversary of Signing of Halifax Resolves	April 12
Confederate Memorial Day	May 10
Memorial Day	Last Monday in May
Anniversary of Mecklenburg Declaration of Independence	May 20
Independence Day	July 4
Labor Day	First Monday in September
Columbus Day and Farmer's Day	Second Monday in October
Yom Kippur	(varies)
Veterans' Day	November 11
Thanksgiving Day	Fourth Thursday in November
Christmas Day	December 25

NOTE: When a legal holiday falls on a Sunday, the next day is considered a legal holiday.

Appendix C
Forms

Use of the following forms is described in the text or should be self-explanatory. If you do not understand any aspect of a form, you should seek advice from an attorney.

Table of Forms

TENANT APPLICATION

Name______________________________ Date of Birth ________________

Name______________________________ Date of Birth ________________

Soc. Sec. Nos.____

Drivers' License Nos.___________________________________

Children & Ages______________________________________

Present Landlord____________________________ Phone______________

Address ________________________________ How Long?____________

Previous Landlord____________________________ Phone______________

Address____

Second Previous Landlord________________________ Phone______________

Address____

Nearest Relative____________________________ Phone______________

Address____

Employer________________________________ Phone______________

Address____

Second Applicant's Employer______________________Phone______________

Address____

Pets____

Other persons who will stay at premises for more than one week________________

____

Bank Name____________________________Acct. #__________________

Bank Name____________________________Acct. #__________________

Have you ever been evicted?____________________________________

Have you ever been in litigation with a landlord?________________________

The undersigned hereby attest that the above information is true.

____

____

INSPECTION REPORT

Date: ____________________

Unit: ____

AREA	CONDITION			
	Move-In		Move-out	
	Good	Poor	Good	Poor
Yard/garden				
Driveway				
Patio/porch				
Exterior				
Entry light/bell				
Living room/Dining room/Halls:				
Floors/carpets				
Walls/ceiling				
Doors/locks				
Fixtures/lights				
Outlets/switches				
Other				
Bedrooms:				
Floors/carpets				
Walls/ceiling				
Doors/locks				
Fixtures/lights				
Outlets/switches				
Other				
Bathrooms:				
Faucets				
Toilet				
Sink/tub				
Floors/carpet				
Walls/ceiling				
Doors/locks				
Fixtures/lights				
Outlets/switches				
Other				
Kitchen:				
Refrigerator				
Range				
Oven				
Dishwasher				
Sink/disposal				
Cabinets/counters				
Floors/carpets				
Walls/ceiling				
Doors/locks				
Fixtures/lights				
Outlets/switches				
Other				
Misc.				
Closets/pantry				
Garage				
Keys				
Other				

PET AGREEMENT

THIS AGREEMENT is made pursuant to that certain Lease dated ________________ between ____ as Landlord and ____ as Tenant.

In consideration of $________ as non-refundable cleaning payment and $________ as additional security deposit paid by Tenant to Landlord, Tenant is allowed to keep the following pet(s): ____
on the premises ____
under the following conditions:

1. In the event the pet produces a litter, Tenant may keep them at the premises no longer than one month past weaning.
2. Tenant shall not engage in any commercial pet-raising activities.
3. No pets other than those listed above shall be kept on the premises without the further written permission of the Landlord.
4. Tenant agrees at all times to keep the pet from becoming a nuisance to neighbors and/or other tenants. This includes controlling the barking of the pet, if necessary and cleaning any animal waste on and about the premises.
5. In the event the pet causes destruction of the property, becomes a nuisance, or Tenant otherwise violates this agreement, Landlord may terminate the Lease according to North Carolina law.

Date: ____________________

Landlord:	Tenant:
______________________________	______________________________
______________________________	______________________________

HOUSE OR DUPLEX LEASE

LANDLORD:_________________________ TENANT:_____________________________

_________________________________ _____________________________

PROPERTY:____

IN CONSIDERATION of the mutual covenants and agreements herein contained, Landlord hereby leases to Tenant and Tenant hereby leases from Landlord the above-described property under the following terms:

1. TERM. This lease shall be for a term of ________________ beginning ___________________, 19___ and ending ___________________, _______.

2. RENT. The rent shall be $________ per ____________ and shall be due on or before the ________ day of each ______________. In the event the rent is received more than five (5) days late, a late charge of $_______ shall be due. In the event a check bounces or an eviction notice must be posted, Tenant agrees to pay a $20.00 charge.

3. PAYMENT. Payment must be received by Landlord on or before the due date at the following address: ____ or such place as designated by Landlord in writing. Tenant understands that this may require early mailing. In the event a check bounces, Landlord may require cash or certified funds.

4. DEFAULT. In the event Tenant defaults under any terms of this lease, Landlord may recover possession as provided by Law and seek monetary damages.

5. SECURITY. Landlord acknowledges receipt of the sum of $__________ as the last month's rent under this lease, plus $__________ as security deposit. In the event Tenant terminates the lease prior to its expiration date, said amounts are non-refundable as a charge for Landlord's trouble in securing a new tenant, but Landlord reserves the right to seek additional damages if they exceed the above amounts.

6. UTILITIES. Tenant agrees to pay all utility charges on the property except: ________________ ___________________.

7. MAINTENANCE. Tenant has examined the property, acknowledges it to be in good repair and in consideration of the reduced rental rate, Tenant agrees to keep the premises in good repair and to do all minor maintenance promptly (under $__________ excluding labor) and provide extermination service.

8. LOCKS. If Tenant adds or changes locks on the premises, Landlord shall be given copies of the keys. Landlord shall at all times have keys for access to the premises in case of emergencies.

9. ASSIGNMENT. This lease may not be assigned by Tenant without the written consent of the Landlord.

10. USE. Tenant shall not use the premises for any illegal purpose or any purpose which will increase the rate of insurance and shall not cause a nuisance for Landlord or neighbors. Tenant shall not create any environmental hazards on the premises.

11. LAWN. Tenant agrees to maintain the lawn and shrubbery on the premises at Tenant's expense.

12. LIABILITY. Tenant shall be responsible for insurance on his own property and agrees not to hold Landlord liable for any damages to Tenant's property on the premises.

13. ACCESS. Landlord reserves the right to enter the premises for the purposes of inspection and to show to prospective purchasers.

14. PETS. No pets shall be allowed on the premises except: ____________________ and there shall be a $___________ non-refundable pet deposit.

15. OCCUPANCY. The premises shall not be occupied by more than _____ adults and _____ children.

16. TENANT'S APPLIANCES. Tenant agrees not to use any heaters, fixtures or appliances drawing excessive current without consent of the Landlord.

17. PARKING. Tenant agrees that no parking is allowed on the premises except: _________

____. No boats, recreation vehicles or disassembled automobiles may be stored on the premises.

18. FURNISHINGS. Any articles provided to Tenant and listed on attached schedule are to be returned in good condition at the termination of this lease.

19. ALTERATIONS AND IMPROVEMENTS. Tenant shall make no alterations to the property without the written consent of the Landlord and any such alterations or improvements shall become the property of the Landlord.

20. ENTIRE AGREEMENT. This lease constitutes the entire agreement between the parties and may not be modified except in writing signed by both parties.

21. HARASSMENT. Tenant shall not do any acts to intentionally harass the Landlord or other tenants.

22. ATTORNEY'S FEES. In the event it becomes necessary to enforce this Agreement through the services of an attorney, Tenant shall be required to pay Landlord's attorney's fees.

23. SEVERABILITY. In the event any section of this Agreement shall be held to be invalid, all remaining provisions shall remain in full force and effect.

24. RECORDING. This lease shall not be recorded in any public records.

25. WAIVER. Any failure by Landlord to exercise any rights under this Agreement shall not constitute a waiver of Landlord's rights.

26. ABANDONMENT. In the event Tenant abandons the property prior to the expiration of the lease, Landlord may relet the premises and hold Tenant liable for any costs, lost rent or damage to the premises. Lessor may dispose of any property abandoned by Tenant.

27. SUBORDINATION. Tenant's interest in the premises shall be subordinate to any encumbrances now or hereafter placed on the premises, to any advances made under such encumbrances, and to any extensions or renewals thereof. Tenant agrees to sign any documents indicating such subordination which may be required by lenders.

28. SURRENDER OF PREMISES. At the expiration of the term of this lease, Tenant shall immediately surrender the premises in as good condition as at the start of this lease.

29. LIENS. The estate of Landlord shall not be subject to any liens for improvements contracted by Tenant.

30. RADON GAS: Radon is a naturally occurring radioactive gas that, when it has accumulated in a building in sufficient quantities, may present health risks to persons who are exposed to it over time. Levels of radon that exceed federal and state guidelines have been found in buildings in North Carolina. Additional information regarding radon and radon testing may be obtained from your county public health unit.

31. SMOKE DETECTORS. Tenant shall be responsible for supplying smoke detectors, for keeping them operational and for changing the battery when needed.

32. ABANDONED PROPERTY. BY SIGNING THIS RENTAL AGREEMENT THE TENANT AGREES THAT UPON SURRENDER OR ABANDONMENT, AS DEFINED BY THE NORTH CAROLINA STATUTES, THE LANDLORD SHALL NOT BE LIABLE OR RESPONSIBLE FOR STORAGE OR DISPOSITION OF THE TENANT'S PERSONAL PROPERTY.

33. MISCELLANEOUS PROVISIONS. ____
____
____
____.

WITNESS the hands and seals of the parties hereto as of this _____ day of ________________, ______.

LANDLORD:	TENANT:
________________________	________________________
________________________	________________________

APARTMENT LEASE

LANDLORD:_________________________ TENANT:_________________________

_________________________ _________________________

PROPERTY:____

IN CONSIDERATION of the mutual covenants and agreements herein contained, Landlord hereby leases to Tenant and Tenant hereby leases from Landlord the above-described property under the following terms:

1. TERM. This lease shall be for a term of _____________ beginning _________________, 19___ and ending _________________, 19___.

2. RENT. The rent shall be $_______ per ___________ and shall be due on or before the _________ day of each _____________. In the event the rent is received more than five (5) days late, a late charge of $_______ shall be due. In the event a check bounces or an eviction notice must be posted, Tenant agrees to pay a $20.00 charge.

3. PAYMENT. Payment must be received by Landlord on or before the due date at the following address: ____ or such place as designated by Landlord in writing. Tenant understands that this may require early mailing. In the event a check bounces, Landlord may require cash or certified funds.

4. DEFAULT. In the event Tenant defaults under any terms of this lease, Landlord may recover possession as provided by Law and seek monetary damages.

5. SECURITY. Landlord acknowledges receipt of the sum of $________ as the last month's rent under this lease, plus $________ as security deposit. In the event Tenant terminates the lease prior to its expiration date, said amounts are non-refundable as a charge for Landlord's trouble in securing a new tenant, but Landlord reserves the right to seek additional damages if they exceed the above amounts.

6. UTILITIES. Tenant agrees to pay all utility charges on the property except: _______________ _________________________________.

7. MAINTENANCE. Tenant has examined the property, acknowledges it to be in good repair. Tenant shall immediately repay any and all damage to the premises caused by Tenant or Tenant's guests. In the event of maintenance problems not caused by Tenant, they shall be immediately reported to Landlord or Landlord's agent.

8. LOCKS. If Tenant adds or changes locks on the premises, Landlord shall be given copies of the keys. Landlord shall at all times have keys for access to the premises in case of emergencies.

9. ASSIGNMENT. This lease may not be assigned by Tenant without the written consent of the Landlord.

10. USE. Tenant shall not use the premises for any illegal purpose or any purpose which will increase the rate of insurance and shall not cause a nuisance for Landlord or neighbors. Tenant shall not create any environmental hazards on the premises.

11. CONDOMINIUM. In the event the premises are a condominium unit, Tenant agrees to abide by all rules, regulations and the declaration of condominium. Maintenance and recreation fees are to be paid by _______________. This lease is subject to approval by the condominium association and Tenant agrees to pay any fees necessary for such approval.

12. LIABILITY. Tenant shall be responsible for insurance on his own property and agrees not to hold Landlord liable for any damages to Tenant's property on the premises.

13. ACCESS. Landlord reserves the right to enter the premises for the purposes of inspection and to show to prospective purchasers.

14. PETS. No pets shall be allowed on the premises except: _________________ and there shall be a $_________ non-refundable pet deposit.

15. OCCUPANCY. The premises shall not be occupied by more than ____ adults and ____ children.

16. TENANT'S APPLIANCES. Tenant agrees not to use any heaters, fixtures or appliances drawing excessive current without consent of the Landlord.

17. PARKING. Tenant agrees that no parking is allowed on the premises except:__________________________ __________________________________. No boats, recreation vehicles or disassembled automobiles may be stored on the premises.

18. FURNISHINGS. Any articles provided to Tenant and listed on attached schedule are to be returned in good condition at the termination of this lease.

19. ALTERATIONS AND IMPROVEMENTS. Tenant shall make no alterations to the property without the written consent of the Landlord and any such alterations or improvements shall become the property of the Landlord.

20. ENTIRE AGREEMENT. This lease constitutes the entire agreement between the parties and may not be modified except in writing signed by both parties.

21. HARASSMENT. Tenant shall not do any acts to intentionally harass the Landlord or other tenants.

22. ATTORNEY'S FEES. In the event it becomes necessary to enforce this Agreement through the services of an attorney, Tenant shall be required to pay Landlord's attorney's fees.

23. SEVERABILITY. In the event any section of this Agreement shall be held to be invalid, all remaining provisions shall remain in full force and effect.

24. RECORDING. This lease shall not be recorded in any public records.

25. WAIVER. Any failure by Landlord to exercise any rights under this Agreement shall not constitute a waiver of Landlord's rights.

26. ABANDONMENT. In the event Tenant abandons the property prior to the expiration of the lease, Landlord may relet the premises and hold Tenant liable for any costs, lost rent or damage to the premises. Lessor may dispose of any property abandoned by Tenant.

27. SUBORDINATION. Tenants interest in the premises shall be subordinate to any encumbrances now or hereafter placed on the premises, to any advances made under such encumbrances, and to any extensions or renewals thereof. Tenant agrees to sign any documents indicating such subordination which may be required by lenders.

28. SURRENDER OF PREMISES. At the expiration of the term of this lease, Tenant shall immediately surrender the premises in as good condition as at the start of this lease.

29. LIENS. The estate of Landlord shall not be subject to any liens for improvements contracted by Tenant.

30. RADON GAS: Radon is a naturally occurring radioactive gas that, when it has accumulated in a building in sufficient quantities, may present health risks to persons who are exposed to it over time. Levels of radon that exceed federal and state guidelines have been found in buildings in North Carolina. Additional information regarding radon and radon testing may be obtained from your county public health unit.

31. SMOKE DETECTORS. Tenant shall be responsible for keeping smoke detectors operational and for changing battery when needed.

32. ABANDONED PROPERTY. BY SIGNING THIS RENTAL AGREEMENT THE TENANT AGREES THAT UPON SURRENDER OR ABANDONMENT, AS DEFINED BY THE NORTH CAROLINA STATUTES, THE LANDLORD SHALL NOT BE LIABLE OR RESPONSIBLE FOR STORAGE OR DISPOSITION OF THE TENANT'S PERSONAL PROPERTY.

33.MISCELLANEOUS PROVISIONS. ____

____

____.

WITNESS the hands and seals of the parties hereto as of this _______ day of ____________________, ______.

LANDLORD: TENANT:

__________________________________ __________________________________

__________________________________ __________________________________

RENTAL AGREEMENT

LANDLORD:_________________________ TENANT:_____________________________

_________________________________ _________________________________

PROPERTY:____

IN CONSIDERATION of the mutual covenants and agreements herein contained, Landlord hereby rents to Tenant and Tenant hereby rents from Landlord the above-described property under the following terms:

1. TERM. This Rental Agreement shall be for a month-to-month tenancy which may be cancelled by either party upon giving notice to the other party at least 7 days prior to the end of a month

2. RENT. The rent shall be $_______ per month and shall be due on or before the ________ day of each month. In the event the rent is received more than five (5) days late, a late charge of $_______ shall be due. In the event a check bounces or an eviction notice must be posted, Tenant agrees to pay a $20.00 charge.

3. PAYMENT. Payment must be received by Landlord on or before the due date at the following address: ____ or such place as designated by Landlord in writing. Tenant understands that this may require early mailing. In the event a check bounces, Landlord may require cash or certified funds.

4. DEFAULT. In the event Tenant defaults under any terms of this agreement, Landlord may recover possession as provided by Law and seek monetary damages.

5. SECURITY. Landlord acknowledges receipt of the sum of $_________ as the last month's rent under this lease, plus $_________ as security deposit against rent or damages. In the event Tenant vacates the premises without giving proper notice, said amounts are non-refundable as a charge for Landlord's trouble in securing a new tenant, but Landlord reserves the right to seek additional payment for any damages to the premises.

6. UTILITIES. Tenant agrees to pay all utility charges on the property except: ________________ _________________________________.

7. MAINTENANCE. Tenant has examined the property, acknowledges it to be in good repair and in consideration of the reduced rental rate, Tenant agrees to keep the premises in good repair and to do all minor maintenance promptly (under $_________ excluding labor) and provide extermination service.

8. LOCKS. If Tenant adds or changes locks on the premises, Landlord shall be given copies of the keys. Landlord shall at all times have keys for access to the premises in case of emergencies.

9. ASSIGNMENT. This agreement may not be assigned by Tenant without the written consent of the Landlord.

10. USE. Tenant shall not use the premises for any illegal purpose or any purpose which will increase the rate of insurance and shall not cause a nuisance for Landlord or neighbors. Tenant shall not create any environmental hazards on the premises.

11. LAWN. Tenant agrees to maintain the lawn and shrubbery on the premises at his expense.

12. LIABILITY. Tenant shall be responsible for insurance on his own property and agrees not to hold Landlord liable for any damages to Tenant's property on the premises.

13. ACCESS. Landlord reserves the right to enter the premises for the purposes of inspection and to show to prospective purchasers.

14. PETS. No pets shall be allowed on the premises except: ___________________ and there shall be a $__________ non-refundable pet deposit.

15. OCCUPANCY. The premises shall not be occupied by more than _____ adults and _____ children.

16. TENANT'S APPLIANCES. Tenant agrees not to use any heaters, fixtures or appliances drawing excessive current without consent of the Landlord.

17. PARKING. Tenant agrees that no parking is allowed on the premises except: ______________ ______________________. No boats, recreation vehicles or disassembled automobiles may be stored on the premises.

18. FURNISHINGS. Any articles provided to tenant and listed on attached schedule are to be returned in good condition at the termination of this agreement.

19. ALTERATIONS AND IMPROVEMENTS. Tenant shall make no alterations to the property without the written consent of the Landlord and any such alterations or improvements shall become the property of the Landlord.

20. ENTIRE AGREEMENT. This rental agreement constitutes the entire agreement between the parties and may not be modified except in writing signed by both parties.

21. HARASSMENT. Tenant shall not do any acts to intentionally harass the Landlord or other tenants.

22. ATTORNEY'S FEES. In the event it becomes necessary to enforce this agreement through the services of an attorney, Tenant shall be required to pay Landlord's attorney's fees.

23. SEVERABILITY. In the event any section of this agreement shall be held to be invalid, all remaining provisions shall remain in full force and effect.

24. RECORDING. This agreement shall not be recorded in any public records.

25. WAIVER. Any failure by Landlord to exercise any rights under this agreement shall not constitute a waiver of Landlord's rights.

26. ABANDONMENT. In the event Tenant abandons the property prior to the expiration of the lease, Landlord may relet the premises and hold Tenant liable for any costs, lost rent or damage to the premises. Lessor may dispose of any property abandoned by Tenant.

27. SUBORDINATION. Tenants interest in the premises shall be subordinate to any encumbrances now or hereafter placed on the premises, to any advances made under such encumbrances, and to any extensions or renewals thereof. Tenant agrees to sign any documents indicating such subordination which may be required by lenders.

28. SURRENDER OF PREMISES. At the expiration of the term of this agreement, Tenant shall immediately surrender the premises in as good condition as at the start of this agreement.

29. LIENS. The estate of Landlord shall not be subject to any liens for improvements contracted by Tenant.

30. RADON GAS: Radon is a naturally occurring radioactive gas that, when it has accumulated in a building in sufficient quantities, may present health risks to persons who are exposed to it over time. Levels of radon that exceed federal and state guidelines have been found in buildings in North Carolina. Additional information regarding radon and radon testing may be from your county public health unit.

31. SMOKE DETECTORS. Tenant shall be responsible for keeping smoke detectors operational and for changing battery when needed.

32. ABANDONED PROPERTY. BY SIGNING THIS RENTAL AGREEMENT THE TENANT AGREES THAT UPON SURRENDER OR ABANDONMENT, AS DEFINED BY THE NORTH CAROLINA STATUTES, THE LANDLORD SHALL NOT BE LIABLE OR RESPONSIBLE FOR STORAGE OR DISPOSITION OF THE TENANT'S PERSONAL PROPERTY.

33.MISCELLANEOUS PROVISIONS. ____ ____.

WITNESS the hands and seals of the parties hereto as of this _____ day of __________________, ______.

LANDLORD: TENANT:

___________________________ ___________________________

___________________________ ___________________________

INSPECTION REQUEST

Date:

To:

It will be necessary to enter your dwelling unit for the purpose of ____________________

____

____. If possible we would like access on ________________________ at ____o'clock ___.m.

In the event this is not convenient, please call to arrange another time.

Sincerely,

____

Landlord's Name______________________

Address ______________________________

____

Phone Number _______________________

STATEMENT FOR REPAIRS

Date:

To:

It has been necessary to repair damage to the premises which you occupy which was caused by you or your guests. The costs for repairs were as follows:

This amount is your responsibility under the terms of the lease and North Carolina law and should be forwarded to us at the address below.

Sincerely,

____

Landlord's Name______________________

Address ______________________________

____

Phone Number ______________________

NOTICE OF CHANGE OF TERMS

Date:

To:

Dear

You are hereby notified that effective ______________________________ the terms of your rental agreement will be changed as follows:

If you elect to terminate your tenancy prior to that date kindly provide 15 days notice as provided by law.

Sincerely,

____

Landlord's Name______________________

Address ____________________________

____

Phone Number _______________________

LETTER TO VACATING TENANT

Date:

To:

Dear ____________________

This letter is to remind you that your lease will expire on ______________________. Please be advised that we do not intend to renew or extend the lease.

The keys should be delivered to us at the address below on or before the end of the lease along with your forwarding address. We will inspect the premises for damages, deduct any amounts necessary for repairs and refund any remaining balance as required by law.

Sincerely,

____

Landlord's Name____________________

Address ___________________________

____

Phone Number _____________________

ANNUAL LETTER—CONTINUATION OF TENANCY

Date:

To:

Dear ___________________

This letter is to remind you that your lease will expire on ___________________. Please advise us within _____ days as to whether you intend to renew your lease. If so, we will prepare a new lease for your signature(s).

If you do not intend to renew your lease, the keys should be delivered to us at the address below on or before the end of the lease along with your forwarding address. We will inspect the premises for damages, deduct any amounts necessary for repairs and refund any remaining balance as required by law.

If we have not heard from you as specified above we will assume that you will be vacating the premises and will arrange for a new tenant to move in at the end of your term.

Sincerely,

____

Landlord's Name______________________

Address ______________________________

____

Phone Number _______________________

NOTICE OF TERMINATION OF AGENT

Date:

To:

You are hereby advised that _________________________ is no longer our agent effective _______________________________. On and after this date he or she is no longer authorized to collect rent, accept notices or to make any representations or agreements regarding the property.

Rent should thereafter be paid to us directly unless you are instructed otherwise by in writing.

If you have any questions you may contact us at the address or phone number below.

Sincerely,

____

Landlord's Name_____________________

Address _____________________________

____

Phone Number ______________________

NOTICE OF APPOINTMENT OF AGENT

Date:

To:

You are hereby advised that effective ____________________________, our agent for collection of rent and other matters regarding the property will be ____________________________. However, no terms of the written lease may be modified or waived without our written signature(s).

If you have any questions you may contact us at the address or phone number below.

Sincerely,

____

Landlord's Name____________________

Address ___________________________

____

Phone Number _____________________

NOTICE OF DISBURSEMENT OF SECURITY DEPOSIT

To: ______________________________
Tenant's Name

____
Address

____
City, State, Zip Code

Date: ______________________________

o Enclosed please find a check in the amount of $_______. These funds represent the amount which was held as your security deposit on the premises located at:
____
____

o The security deposit which was held on the premises located at: ____________
____ will be retained and applied as follows: (Include an itemized list. Insert damage done to the premises or other reason for claiming security deposit)

___ Enclosed is a check in the amount of $ __________ which represents the balance owed to you.

___ There is an outstanding balance of $ _______ which is due upon receipt of this notice.

____
Landlord's Name ________________________
Address ______________________________
____
Phone Number __________________________

DEMAND FOR PAST DUE RENT

To: ______________________________________
Tenant's Name

____
Address

____
City, State, Zip Code

From: ______________________________________

Date: ______________________________________

You are hereby notified that you are indebted to me in the sum of $__________________ for the rent and use of the premises located at ____
____
____
(insert address of leased premises, including county)
North Carolina, now occupied by you and that I demand payment of the rent or possession of the premises.

If you fail to pay the rent or deliver possession of the premises on or before ________________________, legal action will be taken to have you evicted from the premises.

____
Signature

____
Name of Landlord/Property Manager
(Circle one)

____
Address

____
City, State, Zip Code

____
Phone Number

NOTICE OF TERMINATION

(Tenant's Name and Address)

Dear _____________________________:
(Tenant's Name)

You are hereby notified that your lease is terminated immediately. You shall have _____ days from delivery of this letter to vacate the premises. This action is taken because:

____
Landlord's Name_____________________
Address ___________________________
____
Phone Number ______________________

NOTICE OF NON-RENEWAL

(Tenant's Name and Address)

Dear ______________________________:
(Tenant's Name)

You are notified that your tenancy will not be renewed at the end of the present term. You will be expected to vacate the premises on or before ____________________, _______. In the event that you do not vacate the premises by said date, legal action may be taken in which you may be held liable for double rent, court costs and attorney fees.

____

Landlord's Name____________________

Address ___________________________

____

Phone Number ______________________

STATE OF NORTH CAROLINA

______________________ County

File No.

In The General Court Of Justice
☐ District ☐ Superior Court Division

GENERAL
CIVIL ACTION COVER SHEET

☐ **INITIAL FILING** ☐ **SUBSEQUENT FILING**

Rule 5(b), Rules of Practice For Superior and District Courts

Name Of Plaintiff 1	
Tax ID/SSN	
Name Of Plaintiff 2	
Tax ID/SSN	
Name Of Plaintiff 3	
Tax ID/SSN	

VERSUS

Name Of Defendant 1	
Tax ID/SSN	*Summons Submitted* ☐ *Yes* ☐ *No*
Name Of Defendant 2	
Tax ID/SSN	*Summons Submitted* ☐ *Yes* ☐ *No*
Name Of Defendant 3	
Tax ID/SSN	*Summons Submitted* ☐ *Yes* ☐ *No*

Name And Address Of Attorney Or Party, If Not Represented (complete for initial appearance or change of address)

Attorney Bar No.

☐ Initial Appearance in Case ☐ Change of Address

Name Of Firm

Tax ID No.	*Telephone No.*	*FAX No.*

Counsel for
☐ All Plaintiffs ☐ All Defendants ☐ Only *(List party(ies) represented)*

____

☐ Jury Demanded In Pleading
☐ Complex Litigation

☐ Amount in controversy does not exceed $15,000
☐ Stipulate to arbitration

TYPE OF PLEADING

(check all that apply)

☐ Amended Answer/Reply (AMND-Response)
☐ Amended Complaint (AMND)
☐ Answer/Reply (ANSW-Response)
☐ Complaint (COMP)
☐ Confession of Judgment (CNFJ)
☐ Counterclaim vs. (CTCL)
  ☐ All Plaintiffs ☐ Only *(List on back)*
☐ Crossclaim vs. *(List on back)* (CRSS)
☐ Extend Statute of Limitations, Rule 9 (ESOL)
☐ Extend Time For Answer (MEOT-Response)
☐ Extend Time For Complaint (EXCO)
☐ Rule 12 Motion In Lieu Of Answer (MDLA)
☐ Third Party Complaint *(List Third Party Defendants on Back)* (TPCL)
☐ Other: *(specify)*

NOTE: *Small claims are exempt from cover sheets.*

CLAIMS FOR RELIEF FOR:

☐ Administrative Appeal (ADMA)
☐ Appointment of Receiver (APRC)
☐ Attachment/Garnishment (ATTC)
☐ Claim and Delivery (CLMD)
☐ Collection on Account (ACCT)
☐ Condemnation (CNDM)
☐ Contract (CNTR)
☐ Discovery Scheduling Order (DSCH)
☐ Injunction (INJU)
☐ Medical Malpractice (MDML)
☐ Minor Settlement (MSTL)
☐ Money Owed (MNYO)
☐ Negligence - Motor Vehicle (MVNG)
☐ Negligence - Other (NEGO)
☐ Motor Vehicle Lien G.S. 44A (MVLN)
☐ Limited Driving Privilege - *Out-of-State Convictions* (PLDP)
☐ Possession of Personal Property (POPP)
☐ Product Liability (PROD)
☐ Real Property (RLPR)
☐ Specific Performance (SPPR)
☐ Other: *(specify)*

Date	*Signature Of Attorney/Party*

NOTE: *All papers filed in civil actions, special proceedings and estates shall include as the first page of the filing a cover sheet summarizing the critical elements of the filing in a format prescribed by the Administrative Office of the Courts. The Clerk of Superior Court shall require a party to refile any paper which does not include the required cover sheet.*

AOC-CV-751, Rev. 11/96
(Over)

No.	☐ Additional Plaintiff(s)	Tax ID/SSN

No.	☐ Additional Defendant(s) ☐ Third Party Defendant(s)	Tax ID/SSN	Summons Submitted
			☐ *Yes* ☐ *No*
			☐ *Yes* ☐ *No*
			☐ *Yes* ☐ *No*
			☐ *Yes* ☐ *No*
			☐ *Yes* ☐ *No*
			☐ *Yes* ☐ *No*
			☐ *Yes* ☐ *No*
			☐ *Yes* ☐ *No*

Plaintiff(s) Against Whom Counterclaim Asserted

Defendant(s) Against Whom Crossclaim Asserted

AOC-CV-751, Side Two
Rev. 11/96

File No.

COMPLAINT IN SUMMARY EJECTMENT

G.S. 7A-216, 7A-232; Ch. 42, Art. 3 and 7

Name And Address Of Plaintiff

Social Security No./Taxpayer ID No.

County	Telephone No.

VERSUS

Name And Address Of First Defendant

County	Telephone No.

Name And Address Of Second Defendant

County	Telephone No.

Name And Address Of Plaintiff's Attorney Or Agent

STATE OF NORTH CAROLINA

_____________________ County

In The General Court Of Justice
District Court Division-Small Claims

1. The defendant is a resident of the county named above.
2. The defendant entered into possession of premises described below as a lessee of plaintiff.

Description Of Premises (Include Location)			☐ Conventional ☐ Public Housing ☐ Section 8
Rate Of Rent $ per ☐ Month ☐ Week	Date Rent Due	Date Lease Ended	Type Of Lease ☐ Oral ☐ Written

3. ☐ The defendant failed to pay the rent due on the above date and the plaintiff made demand for the rent and waited the 10-day grace period before filing the complaint.
   ☐ The lease period ended on the above date and the defendant is holding over after the end of the lease period.
   ☐ The defendant breached the condition of the lease described below for which re-entry is specified.
   ☐ Criminal activity or other activity has occurred in violation of G.S. 42-63 as specified below.

Description Of Breach/Criminal Activity (give names, dates, places and illegal activity)

4. The plaintiff has demanded possession of the premises from the defendant, who has refused to surrender it, and the plaintiff is entitled to immediate possession.
5. The defendant owes the plaintiff the following:

Description Of Any Property Damage

Amount Of Damage (If Known)	Amount Of Rent Past Due	Total Amount Due
$	$	$

6. I demand to be put in possession of the premises and to recover the total amount listed above and daily rental until entry of judgment plus interest and reimbursement for court costs.

Date	Signature Of Plaintiff/Attorney/Agent

CERTIFICATION WHEN COMPLAINT SIGNED BY AGENT OF PLAINTIFF

I certify that I am an agent of the plaintiff and have actual knowledge of the facts alleged in this Complaint.

Date	Signature

AOC-CVM-201, Rev. 1/98

(Over)

INSTRUCTIONS TO PLAINTIFF OR DEFENDANT

1. The PLAINTIFF must file a small claim action in the county where at least one of the defendants resides.

2. The PLAINTIFF cannot sue in small claims court for more than $3,000.00 excluding interest and costs.

3. The PLAINTIFF must show the complete name and address of the defendant to ensure service on the defendant. If there are two defendants and they reside at different addresses, the plaintiff must include both addresses. The plaintiff must determine if the defendant is a corporation and sue in the complete corporate name. If the business is not a corporation, the plaintiff must determine the owner's name and sue the owner.

4. The PLAINTIFF may serve the defendant(s) by mailing a copy of the summons and complaint by registered or certified mail, return receipt requested, addressed to the party to be served or by paying the costs to have the sheriff serve the summons and complaint. If certified or registered mail is used, the plaintiff must prepare and file a sworn statement with the Clerk of Superior Court proving service by certified mail and must attach to that statement the postal receipt showing that the letter was accepted.

5. In filling out number 3 in the complaint, if the landlord is seeking to remove the tenant for failure to pay rent when there is no written lease, the first block should be checked. (Defendant failed to pay the rent due on the above date and the plaintiff made demand for the rent and waited the ten (10) day grace period before filing the complaint.) If the landlord is seeking to remove the tenant for failure to pay rent when there is a written lease with an automatic forfeiture clause, the third block should be checked. (The defendant breached the condition of the lease described below for which re-entry is specified.) And "failure to pay rent" should be placed in the space for description of the breach. If the landlord is seeking to evict tenant for violating some other condition in the lease, the third block should also be checked. If the landlord is claiming that the term of the lease has ended and the tenant refuses to leave, the second block should be checked. If the landlord is claiming that criminal activity occurred, the fourth block should be checked and the conduct must be described in space provided.

6. The PLAINTIFF must pay advance court costs at the time of filing this Complaint. In the event that judgment is rendered in favor of the plaintiff, court costs may be charged against the defendant.

7. The PLAINTIFF must appear before the magistrate to prove his/her claim.

8. The DEFENDANT may file a written answer, making defense to the claim, in the office of the Clerk of Superior Court. This answer should be accompanied by a copy for the plaintiff and be filed no later than the time set for trial. The filing of the answer DOES NOT relieve the defendant of the need to appear before the magistrate to assert the defendant's defense.

9. The PLAINTIFF or the DEFENDANT may appeal the magistrate's decision in this case. To appeal, notice must be given in open court when the judgment is rendered, or notice may be given in writing to the Clerk of Superior Court within ten (10) days after the judgment is rendered. If notice is given in writing, the appealing party must also serve written notice of appeal on all other parties. The appealing party must PAY to the Clerk of Superior Court the costs of court for appeal within twenty (20) days after the judgment is rendered.

10. This form is supplied in order to expedite the handling of small claims. It is designed to cover the most common claims.

11. **The Clerk or magistrate cannot advise you about your case or assist you in completing this form. If you have any questions, you should consult an attorney.**

AOC-CVM-201, Side Two, Rev. 1/98

NORTH CAROLINA
JUSTICE

IN THE GENERAL COURT OF

______________________ COUNTY ________________ COURT DIVISION
____ CVD ________

_____________________________,
Plaintiff

COMPLAINT

vs.

_____________________________,
Defendant

Plaintiff, as his/her/its claim for relief, alleges and says the following:

1. This is an action seeking to evict a tenant from real property in __________________ County, North Carolina. (Insert county where the rental property is located.)

2. Plaintiff owns the following described real property in said County : _______________

____

(insert legal or street description of rental property including, if applicable, unit number.)

3. Defendant has possession of the property under a/an (oral/written) agreement to pay rent of $__________ payable__________________ (insert terms of rental payments, i.e. weekly, monthly, etc.). A copy of the written agreement, if any, is attached as Exhibit "A."

4. Defendant failed to pay the rent due on ___________________________. (insert date of payment Tenant has failed to make.)

5. Plaintiff served Defendant with notice on ____________________, _______, (insert date of notice) to pay the rent or deliver possession but Defendant refused to do either. A copy of the notice is attached as Exhibit "B".

6. Defendant owes Plaintiff $ ____________ (insert payment due rent amount) that is due with interest since __________________, ________ (insert date of last rental payment tenant failed to make.)

WHEREFORE, Plaintiff prays the Court for relief as follows:

1. The foregoing Complaint be allowed and taken as an Affidavit in support of the Plaintiff's application for eviction and past due rental payments, and that said Complaint also be allowed and taken as an affidavit upon which to base all orders of the Court.

2. An Order be entered granting the Plaintiff possession of the property against the Defendant and past due rental payments.

3. The Court grant such other and further relief as it deems just and proper.

This the ___________ day of ______________________, _______.

____

Landlord's Name

Address ______________________________

____

Telephone Number ____________________

NORTH CAROLINA ____ CVD ________

______________________________ COUNTY

VERIFICATION

I, ____, being first duly sworn, depose and say: That I an the Plaintiff in this action; that I have read the foregoing ________________________ and know the contents thereof; that the same is true of my own knowledge, save and except those matters and things therein stated upon information and belief, and as to those matters and things, I believe them to be true.

This the __________ day of ____________________, ________.

____

AFFIANT

Sworn to and subscribed before me
this the _____ day of ______________, ______.

____

NOTARY PUBLIC
My Commission Expires:

STATE OF NORTH CAROLINA

File No.

______________ County

In The General Court Of Justice
District Court Division-Small Claims

Plaintiff(s)

VERSUS

Defendant(s)

MAGISTRATE SUMMONS

☐ **ALIAS AND PLURIES SUMMONS**

G.S. 7A-217, -232; 1A-1, Rule 4

Date Last Summons Issued

TO:	TO:
Name And Address Of Defendant 1	*Name And Address Of Defendant 2*

A Small Claim Action Has Been Commenced Against You!

You are notified to appear before the magistrate at the specified date, time and location of trial listed below. You will have the opportunity at the trial to defend yourself against the claim stated in the attached complaint.

You may file a written answer, making defense to the claim, in the office of the Clerk of Superior Court at any time before the time set for trial. Whether or not you file an answer, the plaintiff must prove the claim before the magistrate.

If you fail to appear and defend against the proof offered, the magistrate may enter a judgment against you.

Date of Trial	*Time Of Trial* ☐ AM ☐ PM	*Location Of Court*
Name And Address Of Plaintiff Or Plaintiff's Attorney		*Date Issued*
		Signature
		☐ *Deputy CSC* ☐ *Assistant CSC* ☐ *Clerk Of Superior Court*

AOC-CVM-100, Rev. 3/98

(Over)

RETURN OF SERVICE

I certify that this Summons and a copy of the complaint were received and served as follows:

DEFENDANT 1

Date Served	*Name Of Defendant*

☐ By delivering to the defendant named above a copy of the summons and complaint.

☐ By leaving a copy of summons and complaint at the dwelling house or usual place of abode of the defendant named above with a person of suitable age and discretion then residing therein.

☐ As the defendant is a corporation, service was effected by delivering a copy of the summons and complaint to the person named below.

Name And Address Of Person With Whom Copy Left (If Corporation, Give Title Of Person Copy Left With)

☐ Other manner of service: *(specify).*

☐ Defendant WAS NOT served for the following reason:

DEFENDANT 2

Date Served	*Name Of Defendant*

☐ By delivering to the defendant named above a copy of the summons and complaint.

☐ By leaving a copy of summons and complaint at the dwelling house or usual place of abode of the defendant named above with a person of suitable age and discretion then residing therein.

☐ As the defendant is a corporation, service was effected by delivering a copy of the summons and complaint to the person named below.

Name And Address Of Person With Whom Copy Left (If Corporation, Give Title Of Person Copy Left With)

☐ Other manner of service: *(specify).*

☐ Defendant WAS NOT served for the following reason:

FOR USE IN SUMMARY EJECTMENT CASES ONLY

☐ Service was made by mailing by first class mail a copy of the summons and complaint to the defendant(s) and by posting a copy of the summons and complaint at the following premises.

Date Served	*Name(s) Of The Defendant(s) Served By Posting*

Address Of Premises Where Posted

Service Fee	*Date Received*	*Name Of Sheriff*
$		
By	*Date Of Return*	*County*
		Deputy Sheriff Making Return

AOC-CVM-100, Rev. 3/98

STATE OF NORTH CAROLINA	File No.
_____________ County	In The General Court Of Justice ☐ District ☐ Superior Court Division

Name Of Plaintiff	
Address	**CIVIL SUMMONS**
City, State, Zip	
VERSUS	G.S. 1A-1, Rules 3, 4
Name Of Defendant(s)	☐ Alias and Pluries Summons Date Last Summons Issued

To Each Of The Defendant(s) Named Below:

Name And Address Of Defendant 1	Name And Address Of Defendant 2

A Civil Action Has Been Commenced Against You!

You are notified to appear and answer the complaint of the plaintiff as follows:

1. Serve a copy of your written answer to the complaint upon the plaintiff or plaintiff's attorney within thirty (30) days after you have been served. You may serve your answer by delivering a copy to the plaintiff or by mailing it to the plaintiff's last known address, and
2. File the original of the written answer with the Clerk of Superior Court of the county named above.

If you fail to answer the complaint, the plaintiff will apply to the Court for the relief demanded in the complaint.

Name And Address Of Plaintiff's Attorney (If None, Address Of Plaintiff)	Date Issued	Time ☐ AM ☐ PM
	Signature	
	☐ Deputy CSC ☐ Assistant CSC ☐ Clerk Of Superior Court	

☐ ENDORSEMENT	Date Of Endorsement	Time ☐ AM ☐ PM
This Summons was originally issued on the date indicated above and returned not served. At the request of the plaintiff, the time within which this Summons must be served is extended thirty (30) days.	Signature	
	☐ Deputy CSC ☐ Assistant CSC ☐ Clerk Of Superior Court	

NOTE TO PARTIES: *Many counties have **MANDATORY ARBITRATION** programs in which most cases where the amount in controversy is $15,000 or less are heard by an arbitrator before a trial. The parties will be notified if this case is assigned for mandatory arbitration, and, if so, what procedure is to be followed.*

AOC-CV-100
Rev. 9/96

(Over)

RETURN OF SERVICE

I certify that this Summons and a copy of the complaint were received and served as follows:

DEFENDANT 1

Date Served	*Name Of Defendant*

☐ By delivering to the defendant named above a copy of the summons and complaint.

☐ By leaving a copy of the summons and complaint at the dwelling house or usual place of abode of the defendant named above with a person of suitable age and discretion then residing therein.

☐ As the defendant is a corporation, service was effected by delivering a copy of the summons and complaint to the person named below.

Name And Address Of Person With Whom Copies Left (if corporation, give title of person copies left with)

☐ Other manner of service *(specify)*

☐ Defendant WAS NOT served for the following reason:

DEFENDANT 2

Date Served	*Name Of Defendant*

☐ By delivering to the defendant named above a copy of the summons and complaint.

☐ By leaving a copy of the summons and complaint at the dwelling house or usual place of abode of the defendant named above with a person of suitable age and discretion then residing therein.

☐ As the defendant is a corporation, service was effected by delivering a copy of the summons and complaint to the person named below.

Name And Address Of Person With Whom Copies Left (if corporation, give title of person copies left with)

☐ Other manner of service *(specify)*

☐ Defendant WAS NOT served for the following reason.

Service Fee Paid	*Date Received*	*Name Of Sheriff*
Paid By	*Date Of Return*	*County*
		Deputy Sheriff Making Return

AOC-CV-100, Side Two
Rev. 9/96

NORTH CAROLINA

______________________ COUNTY

IN THE GENERAL COURT OF JUSTICE

________________ COURT DIVISION

___ CVD ________

______________________________,
Plaintiff

vs.

______________________________,
Defendant

AFFIDAVIT OF DAMAGES

I, ____________________________________ being first duly sworn, depose and say:

1. I am ___ the Plaintiff or ___ the Plaintiff's agent (check appropriate response) in this case and am authorized to make this affidavit.

2. This affidavit is based on my own personal knowledge.

3. Defendant has possession of the property which is the subject of this eviction under an agreement to pay rent of $ _________ (rental amount) per ___________ (week, month, or other payment period).

4. Defendant has not paid the rent due since ____________________, ________ (date of payment tenant has failed to make).

5. Defendant owes Plaintiff $ ________________ (past due rent amount) as alleged in the complaint plus interest.

6. Defendant owes Plaintiff $ _________________ (amount of other damages) as alleged in the complaint plus interest.

____
Name

Sworn to and subscribed before me
this the _______ day of ______________, _____.

____
Notary Public
My Commission Expires:

NORTH CAROLINA

______________________ COUNTY

IN THE GENERAL COURT OF JUSTICE

_______________ COURT DIVISION

____ CVD _______

______________________________,
Plaintiff

vs.

______________________________,
Defendant

NOTICE OF HEARING

PLEASE TAKE NOTICE that the undersigned will bring the ____________________ ____________________ for hearing before the court at ______________________, North Carolina on the _______ day of _________________, ________ at _________ _____.M in Courtroom ________, or as soon thereafter as the court can hear it.

This the _____ day of _______________, _______.

____
Plaintiff's Name
Address:___________________________
____
Telephone No. ______________________

CERTIFICATE OF SERVICE

I, ___________________________, certify that a copy of the NOTICE OF HEARING was served upon the opposing party or his/her attorney by depositing a copy of the same in the United States mail with pre-paid, first-class postage, and addressed as follows:

This the______ day of __________________, _______.

____
Name

NOTICE OF RIGHT TO RECLAIM ABANDONED PROPERTY
(Property of former tenant valued under $100)

To: ______________________________
____
____

WHEN YOU VACATED THE PREMISES AT ______________________________, APT. __________, THE FOLLOWING PERSONAL PROPERTY REMAINED:

YOU MAY CLAIM THIS PROPERTY AT ____________________________________
____
UNLESS YOU PAY THE REASONABLE COST OF STORAGE AND ADVERTISING, IF ANY, FOR ALL THE ABOVE-DESCRIBED PROPERTY AND TAKE POSSESSION OF THE PROPERTY WHICH YOU CLAIM NO LATER THAN ____________________________________.
*THIS PROPERTY MAY BE DISPOSED OF PURSUANT TO N.C.G.S. 42-25.9(h).

BECAUSE THE PROPERTY IS BELIEVED TO BE WORTH LESS THAN $100, IT MAY BE KEPT, SOLD, OR DESTROYED WITHOUT FURTHER NOTICE IF YOU FAIL TO RECLAIM IT WITHIN THE TIME INDICATED ABOVE.

Dated: ______________________

____
Landlord

Telephone____________________________

Address: ____________________________
____
____

* Insert date not fewer than 5 days after notice is personally delivered or, if mailed, not fewer than 10 days after notice is deposited in the mail.

NOTICE OF RIGHT TO RECLAIM ABANDONED PROPERTY
(Property of former tenant valued $500 or less)

To: ________________________________
____
____

WHEN YOU VACATED THE PREMISES AT ____________________________________, APT. ______________, YOU FAILED TO REMOVE YOUR PERSONAL PROPERTY. (DO NOT INCLUDE A DESCRIPTION OF THE PERSONAL PROPERTY.)

YOU MAY CLAIM THIS PROPERTY AT: ____
____
(Include the name and address of the charitable organization.)

UNLESS YOU RECLAIM AND TAKE POSSESSION OF THE PROPERTY NO LATER THAN ______________________________* THIS PROPERTY MAY BE DISPOSED OF PURSUANT TO N.C.G.S 42-25.9(b).

Dated: ________________________

____
Landlord

Telephone:_____________________________

Address: ______________________________
____

* Insert date not fewer than 30 days after notice is personally delivered or, if mailed, not fewer than 35 days after notice is deposited in the mail.

NOTICE OF SALE OF ABANDONED PROPERTY

To: ______________________________
____
____

WHEN YOU VACATED THE PREMISES AT ____________________________________, APT. ________, YOU FAILED TO REMOVE YOUR PERSONAL PROPERTY.

YOUR ABANDONED PROPERTY SHALL BE SOLD ON ____________________ (DATE)* at __________________ (TIME). THE SALE SHALL TAKE PLACE AT ____ (LOCATION OF SALE).

IF YOU REQUEST THE PROPERTY PRIOR TO THE DAY OF THE SALE, IT SHALL BE RETURNED TO YOU.

ANY SURPLUS OF PROCEEDS FROM THE SALE, AFTER PAYMENT OF UNPAID RENTS, DAMAGES, STORAGE FEES AND SALE COSTS, SHALL BE RETURNED TO YOU IF REQUESTED WITHIN 10 DAYS AFTER SALE. IF YOU DO NOT REQUEST THE SURPLUS PROCEEDS, IT SHALL BE DELIVERED TO THE GOVERNMENT OF THE COUNTY IN WHICH THE RENTAL PROPERTY IS LOCATED.

Dated: ______________________

____
Landlord

Telephone: ______________________

Address: ________________________
____

*Insert date not fewer than 7 days prior to the sale if notice is personally delivered or, if mailed, not fewer than 12 days after notice is deposited in the mail.

Disclosure of Information on Lead-Based Paint and/or Lead-Based Paint Hazards

Lead Warning Statement
Housing built before 1978 may contain lead-based paint. Lead from paint, paint chips, and dust can pose health hazards if not managed properly. Lead exposure is especially harmful to young children and pregnant women. Before renting pre-1978 housing, lessors must disclose the presence of known lead-based paint and/or lead-based paint hazards in the dwelling. Lessees must also receive a federally approved pamphlet on lead poisoning prevention.

Lessor's Disclosure
(a) Presence of lead-based paint and/or lead-based paint hazards (Check (i) or (ii) below):
(i)_____ Known lead-based paint and/or lead-based paint hazards are present in the housing (explain).

____

(ii)_____ Lessor has no knowledge of lead-based paint and/or lead-based paint hazards in the housing.
(b) Records and reports available to the lessor (Check (i) or (ii) below):
(i)_____ Lessor has provided the lessee with all available records and reports pertaining to lead-based paint and/or lead-based paint hazards in the housing (list documents below).

____

(ii)_____ Lessor has no reports or records pertaining to lead-based paint and/or lead-based paint hazards in the housing.

Lessee's Acknowledgment (initial)
(c)_____ Lessee has received copies of all information listed above.
(d)_____ Lessee has received the pamphlet Protect Your Family from Lead in Your Home.

Agent's Acknowledgment (initial)
(e)_____ Agent has informed the lessor of the lessor's obligations under 42 U.S.C. 4852d and is aware of his/her responsibility to ensure compliance.

Certification of Accuracy
The following parties have reviewed the information above and certify, to the best of their knowledge, that the information they have provided is true and accurate.

______________	______________	______________	______________
Lessor	Date	Lessor	Date
______________	______________	______________	______________
Lessee	Date	Lessee	Date
______________	______________	______________	______________
Agent	Date	Agent	Date

NOTICE OF HOLDING SECURITY DEPOSIT

To: ______________________________

From: ____________________________

Pursuant to North Carolina General Statutes Section 42-50 this notice is to advise you that your security deposit is being held as follows:

Name of Bank/Financial Institution: ______________________________________
____

Address of Bank/Financial Institution: ____________________________________
____

Name of Insurance Company Providing the Bond: _____________________________
____

North Carolina statutes provide as follows:

Section 42-50. Security deposits from the tenant in residential dwelling units shall be deposited in a trust account with a licensed and insured bank or savings institution located in the State of North Carolina or the landlord may, at his option, furnish a bond from an insurance company licensed to do business in North Carolina. The security deposits from the tenant may be held in a trust account outside of the State of North Carolina only if the landlord provides the tenant with an adequate bond in the amount of said deposits. The landlord or his agent shall notify the tenant within 30 days after the beginning of the lease term of the name and address of the bank or institution where his deposit is currently located or the name of the insurance company providing the bond.

Section 42-51. Security deposits for residential dwelling units shall be permitted only for the tenant's possible nonpayment of rent, damage to the premises, nonfulfillment of rental period, any unpaid bill which become a lien against the demised property due to the tenant's occupancy, costs of re-renting the premises after breach by the tenant, costs of removal and storage of tenant's property after a summary ejectment proceeding or court costs in connection with terminating a tenancy. Such security deposit shall not exceed an amount equal to two weeks' rent if a tenancy is week to week, one and one-half months' rent if a tenancy is month to month, and two months' rent for terms greater than month to month. These deposits must be fully accounted for by the landlord as set forth in G.S. 42-52.

Section 42-52. Upon termination of the tenancy, money held by the landlord as security may be applied as permitted in G.S. 42-51 or, if not so applied, shall be refunded to the tenant. In either case the landlord in writing shall itemize any damage and mail or deliver same to the tenant, together with the balance of the security deposit, no later than 30 days after termination of the tenancy and delivery of possession by the tenant. If the tenant's address is unknown the landlord shall apply the deposit as permitted in G.S. 42-51 after a period of 30 days and the landlord shall hold the balance of the deposit for collection by the tenant for at least six months. The landlord may not withhold as damages part of the security deposit for conditions that are due to normal wear and tear nor may the landlord retain an amount from the security deposit which exceeds his actual damages.

AMENDMENT TO LEASE/RENTAL AGREEMENT

The undersigned parties to that certain agreement dated ______________________, ______ on the premises known as ____, ____________________________________ hereby agree to amend said agreement as follows:

WITNESS the hands and seals of the parties hereto this _______ day of __________________, _______.

Landlord: Tenant:

______________________________________ ______________________________________

______________________________________ ______________________________________

NORTH CAROLINA	IN THE GENERAL COURT OF JUSTICE
______________ COUNTY	______________ COURT DIVISION
	_____ CVD ________

______________________________,)
Plaintiff)
)
vs.)
______________________________,)
Defendant)

AFFIDAVIT OF SERVICE BY REGISTERED OR CERTIFIED MAIL

I, ______________________________, duly sworn, depose and say:
Service of process by Certified mail, return receipt requested, has been completed on the Defendant, ______________________________.

This affidavit is filed pursuant to the requirements of North Carolina Rules of Civil Procedure 4 (j2) (2).

1. A copy of the Summons and Complaint was deposited in the Post Office for mailing by certified mail, return receipt requested, and addressed and dispatched to the Defendant.

2. It was mailed to ______________________________, at ______________________, ________________, NC __________.

3. Service was received on ______________________ by the Defendant as evidenced by the attached green return receipt card and completed pursuant to the requirements of N.C.G.S. 1-75.10 (4).

This the _______ day of ________________, _______.

____
(Your Name)

SWORN TO AND SUBSCRIBED BEFORE ME
This the ______ day of ______________, ________.

____
Notary Public
My Commission Expires: ________________

File No.

COMPLAINT FOR MONEY OWED

G.S. 7A-216, 7A-232

Name And Address Of Plaintiff

Social Security No./Taxpayer ID No.

County	Telephone No.

VERSUS

Name And Address Of First Defendant

County	Telephone No.

Name And Address Of Second Defendant

County	Telephone No.

Name And Address Of Plaintiff's Attorney

STATE OF NORTH CAROLINA

_______________ County

In The General Court Of Justice
District Court Division-Small Claims

1. The defendant is a resident of the county named above.
2. The defendant owes me the amount listed for the following reason:

Principal Amount Owed	$
Interest Owed *(if any)*	$
Total Amount Owed	$

(check one below)

☐ On An Account *(attach a copy of the account)*	Date From Which Interest Due		Interest Rate
☐ For Goods Sold And Delivered Between	Beginning Date	Ending Date	Interest Rate
☐ For Money Lent	Date From Which Interest Due		Interest Rate
☐ On a Promissory Note *(attach copy)*	Date Of Note	Date From Which Interest Due	Interest Rate

☐ For a Worthless Check *(attach a copy of the check)*

☐ For conversion *(describe property)*

☐ Other: *(specify)*

I demand to recover the total amount listed above, plus interest and reimbursement for court costs.

Date	Signature Of Plaintiff Or Attorney

AOC-CVM-200, Rev. 1/98

(Over)

INSTRUCTIONS TO PLAINTIFF OR DEFENDANT

1. The PLAINTIFF must file a small claim action in the county where at least one of the defendants resides.

2. The PLAINTIFF cannot sue in small claims court for more than $3,000.00 excluding interest and costs.

3. The PLAINTIFF must show the complete name and address of the defendant to ensure service on the defendant. If there are two defendants and they reside at different addresses, the plaintiff must include both addresses. The plaintiff must determine if the defendant is a corporation and sue in the complete corporate name. If the business is not a corporation, the plaintiff must determine the owner's name and sue the owner.

4. The PLAINTIFF may serve the defendant(s) by mailing a copy of the summons and complaint by registered or certified mail, return receipt requested, addressed to the party to be served or by paying the costs to have the sheriff serve the summons and complaint. If certified or registered mail is used, the plaintiff must prepare and file a sworn statement with the Clerk of Superior Court proving service by certified mail and must attach to that statement the postal receipt showing that the letter was accepted.

5. The PLAINTIFF must pay advance court costs at the time of filing this Complaint. In the event that judgment is rendered in favor of the plaintiff, court costs may be charged against the defendant.

6. The DEFENDANT may file a written answer, making defense to the claim, in the office of the Clerk of Superior Court. This answer should be accompanied by a copy for the plaintiff and be filed no later than the time set for trial. The filing of the answer DOES NOT relieve the defendant of the need to appear before the magistrate to assert the defendant's defense.

   Whether or not an answer is filed, the PLAINTIFF must appear before the magistrate.

7. The PLAINTIFF or the DEFENDANT may appeal the magistrate's decision in this case. To appeal, notice must be given in open court when the judgment is rendered, or notice may be given in writing to the Clerk of Superior Court within ten (10) days after the judgment is rendered. If notice is given in writing, the appealing party must also serve written notice of appeal on all other parties. The appealing party must PAY to the Clerk of Superior Court the costs of court for appeal within twenty (20) days after the judgment is rendered.

8. This form is supplied in order to expedite the handling of small claims. It is designed to cover the most common claims.

9. **The Clerk or magistrate cannot advise you about your case or assist you in completing this form. If you have any questions, you should consult an attorney.**

AOC-CVM-200, Side Two, Rev. 1/98

STATE OF NORTH CAROLINA

_______________________ County

File No.

Judgment Book & Page No. In Original County

In The General Court Of Justice

Name And Address Of Plaintiff

WRIT OF POSSESSION
REAL PROPERTY

G.S. 1-313(4); 42-36.2

VERSUS

Name And Address Of Defendant 1

Name And Address Of Second Defendant 2

To The Sheriff Of ________________________________ **County:**

A judgment in favor of the plaintiff was rendered in this case for the possession of the real property described below; and you are commanded to remove the defendant(s) from, and put the plaintiff in possession of those premises.

Description Of Property (include location)

Date Of Judgment	Date Writ Issued
	Signature
	☐ Deputy CSC ☐ Assistant CSC ☐ Clerk Of Superior Court

AOC-CV-401
Rev. 4/97

(Over)

RETURN OF SERVICE

☐ 1. This Writ Of Possession was served as follows:

- ☐ a. By removing the defendant(s) from the premises and putting the plaintiff in possession after giving notice of removal to the defendant(s) as required by law.
- ☐ b. By removing the defendant(s) from the premises and putting the plaintiff in possession after giving notice of removal to the defendant(s) as required by law. The defendant's(s') property was taken to the warehouse listed below for storage.
- ☐ c. By giving notice of removal to the defendant(s) as required by law and by leaving the defendant's(s') property on the premises and locking the premises in accordance with the written request of the plaintiff which is attached.

☐ 2. I have failed to remove the defendant(s) from the premises for the following reason:

- ☐ a. The plaintiff requested that the Writ be returned because the defendant(s) satisfied the obligation to the plaintiff.
- ☐ b. The plaintiff failed to advance the expenses of removal and one month's storage after being asked to do so.
- ☐ c. Other *(specify)*

Name And Address Of Warehouse

Fee Paid	*Date Received*	*Name Of Sheriff*
$		
Fee Paid By	*Date Executed*	*County*
	Date Returned	*Deputy Sheriff Making Return*

AOC-CV-401, Side Two
Rev. 4/97

RETURN O[illegible]

Writ Of Possession [illegible]

[illegible] the [illegible]
[illegible] of [illegible] (s) [illegible]

b. By [illegible] the defendant(s) from the [illegible]
[illegible] defendant(s) [illegible] defendant [illegible]
were not listed below [illegible]

c. By giving notice of [illegible] to the defendant(s) [illegible]
[illegible] the [illegible]
[illegible]

I have failed to remove the defendant(s) [illegible]

a. The plaintiff [illegible]
[illegible]

The [illegible]

INDEX

S

T

U

V

W

Your #1 Source for Real World Legal Information...

SPHINX® PUBLISHING

A Division of Sourcebooks, Inc.®

- Written by lawyers
- Simple English explanation of the law
- Forms and instructions included

How to Start a Business in North Carolina, 2nd ed.

Essential information on matters crucial to beginning a business in North Carolina. This book includes necessary forms and instructions.

224 pages; $16.95;
ISBN 1-57248-096-3

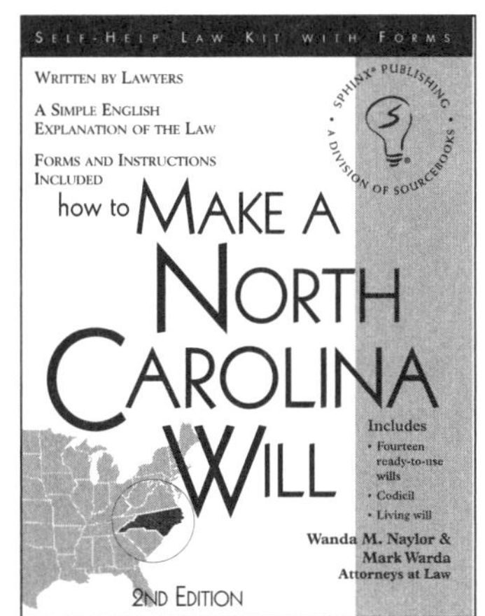

How to make a North Carolina Will, 2nd ed.

Ready-to-use forms and instructions that take care of the many issues, such as inheritance laws, joint property, pay on death accounts and living wills.

128 pages; $12.95;
ISBN 1-57071-327-8

How to Negotiate Real Estate Contracts, 3rd ed.

Do you understand every clause in a real estate contract? A standard form contract can cost you thousands of dollars in unnecessary expenses. This book explains the pitfalls and shows you how you can save money.

128 pages; $16.95;
ISBN 1-57071-331-6

See the following order form for books written specifically for California, Florida, Georgia, Illinois, Massachusetts, Michigan, Minnesota, New York, North Carolina, Pennsylvania, and Texas! *Coming soon—Ohio and New Jersey!*

What our customers say about our books:

"It couldn't be more clear for the lay person." —R.D.

"I want you to know I really appreciate your book. It has saved me a lot of time and money." —L.T.

"Your real estate contracts book has saved me nearly $12,000.00 in closing costs over the past year." —A.B.

"...many of the legal questions that I have had over the years were answered clearly and concisely through your plain English interpretation of the law." —C.E.H.

"If there weren't people out there like you I'd be lost. You have the best books of this type out there." —S.B.

"...your forms and directions are easy to follow." —C.V.M.

Sphinx Publishing's Legal Survival Guides
are directly available from the Sourcebooks, Inc., or from your local bookstores.
For credit card orders call 1–800–43–BRIGHT, write P.O. Box 372, Naperville, IL 60566, or fax 630-961-2168

SPHINX® PUBLISHING ORDER FORM

BILL TO:		SHIP TO:	
Phone #	Terms	F.O.B. Chicago, IL	Ship Date

Charge my: ❒ VISA ❒ MasterCard ❒ American Express

❒ Money Order or Personal Check

Credit Card Number

Expiration Date

Qty	ISBN	Title	Retail	Ext.
		SPHINX PUBLISHING NATIONAL TITLES		
	1-57071-166-6	Crime Victim's Guide to Justice	$19.95	
	1-57071-342-1	Debtors' Rights (3E)	$12.95	
	1-57071-162-3	Defend Yourself against Criminal Charges	$19.95	
	1-57248-082-3	Grandparents' Rights (2E)	$19.95	
	1-57248-087-4	Guia de Inmigracion a Estados Unidos (2E)	$19.95	
	1-57248-103-X	Help Your Lawyer Win Your Case (2E)	$12.95	
	1-57071-164-X	How to Buy a Condominium or Townhome	$16.95	
	1-57071-223-9	How to File Your Own Bankruptcy (4E)	$19.95	
	1-57071-224-7	How to File Your Own Divorce (3E)	$19.95	
	1-57248-083-1	How to Form a Limited Liability Company	$19.95	
	1-57248-099-8	How to Form a Nonprofit Corporation	$24.95	
	1-57071-227-1	How to Form Your Own Corporation (2E)	$19.95	
	1-57071-343-X	How to Form Your Own Partnership	$19.95	
	1-57071-228-X	How to Make Your Own Will	$12.95	
	1-57071-331-6	How to Negotiate Real Estate Contracts (3E)	$16.95	
	1-57071-332-4	How to Negotiate Real Estate Leases (3E)	$16.95	
	1-57071-225-5	How to Register Your Own Copyright (2E)	$19.95	
	1-57248-104-8	How to Register Your Own Trademark (3E)	$19.95	
	1-57071-349-9	How to Win Your Unemployment Compensation Claim	$19.95	
	1-57071-167-4	How to Write Your Own Living Will	$9.95	
	1-57071-344-8	How to Write Your Own Premarital Agreement (2E)	$19.95	
	1-57071-333-2	Jurors' Rights (2E)	$9.95	
	1-57248-032-7	Legal Malpractice and Other Claims against...	$18.95	
	1-57071-400-2	Legal Research Made Easy (2E)	$14.95	
	1-57071-336-7	Living Trusts and Simple Ways to Avoid Probate (2E)	$19.95	
	1-57071-345-6	Most Valuable Bus. Legal Forms You'll Ever Need (2E)	$19.95	
	1-57071-346-4	Most Valuable Corporate Forms You'll Ever Need (2E)	$24.95	
	1-57248-089-0	Neighbor v. Neighbor (2E)	$12.95	
	1-57071-348-0	The Power of Attorney Handbook (3E)	$19.95	
	1-57248-020-3	Simple Ways to Protect Yourself from Lawsuits	$24.95	
	1-57071-337-5	Social Security Benefits Handbook (2E)	$14.95	
	1-57071-163-1	Software Law (w/diskette)	$29.95	
	0-913825-86-7	Successful Real Estate Brokerage Mgmt.	$19.95	
	1-57248-098-X	The Nanny and Domestic Help Legal Kit	$19.95	
	1-57071-399-5	Unmarried Parents' Rights	$19.95	
	1-57071-354-5	U.S.A. Immigration Guide (3E)	$19.95	
	0-913825-82-4	Victims' Rights	$12.95	
	1-57071-165-8	Winning Your Personal Injury Claim	$19.95	
	1-57248-097-1	Your Right to Child Custody, Visitation and Support	$19.95	
		CALIFORNIA TITLES		
	1-57071-360-X	CA Power of Attorney Handbook	$12.95	
	1-57071-355-3	How to File for Divorce in CA	$19.95	
	1-57071-356-1	How to Make a CA Will	$12.95	
	1-57071-408-8	How to Probate an Estate in CA	$19.95	
	1-57071-357-X	How to Start a Business in CA	$16.95	
	1-57071-358-8	How to Win in Small Claims Court in CA	$14.95	
	1-57071-359-6	Landlords' Rights and Duties in CA	$19.95	
		NEW YORK TITLES		
	1-57071-184-4	How to File for Divorce in NY	$19.95	
		FLORIDA TITLES		
	1-57071-363-4	Florida Power of Attorney Handbook (2E)	$12.95	
	1-57248-093-9	How to File for Divorce in FL (6E)	$21.95	
	1-57248-086-6	How to Form a Limited Liability Co. in FL	$19.95	
	1-57071-401-0	How to Form a Partnership in FL	$19.95	
	1-57071-380-4	How to Form a Corporation in FL (4E)	$19.95	
	1-57071-361-8	How to Make a FL Will (5E)	$12.95	
	1-57248-088-2	How to Modify Your FL Divorce Judgment (4E)	$22.95	

Form Continued on Following Page **SUBTOTAL**

To order, call Sourcebooks at 1-800-43-BRIGHT or FAX (630)961-2168 (Bookstores, libraries, wholesalers—please call for discount)

SPHINX® PUBLISHING ORDER FORM

Qty	ISBN	Title	Retail	Ext.
		FLORIDA TITLES (CONT'D)		
____	1-57071-364-2	How to Probate an Estate in FL (3E)	$24.95	____
____	1-57248-081-5	How to Start a Business in FL (5E)	$16.95	____
____	1-57071-362-6	How to Win in Small Claims Court in FL (6E)	$14.95	____
____	1-57071-335-9	Landlords' Rights and Duties in FL (7E)	$19.95	____
____	1-57071-334-0	Land Trusts in FL (5E)	$24.95	____
____	0-913825-73-5	Women's Legal Rights in FL	$19.95	____
		GEORGIA TITLES		
____	1-57071-376-6	How to File for Divorce in GA (3E)	$19.95	____
____	1-57248-075-0	How to Make a GA Will (3E)	$12.95	____
____	1-57248-076-9	How to Start a Business in Georgia (3E)	$16.95	____
		ILLINOIS TITLES		
____	1-57071-405-3	How to File for Divorce in IL (2E)	$19.95	____
____	1-57071-415-0	How to Make an IL Will (2E)	$12.95	____
____	1-57071-416-9	How to Start a Business in IL (2E)	$16.95	____
____	1-57248-078-5	Landlords' Rights & Duties in IL	$19.95	____
		MASSACHUSETTS TITLES		
____	1-57071-329-4	How to File for Divorce in MA (2E)	$19.95	____
____	1-57248-108-0	How to Make a MA Will (2E)	$12.95	____
____	1-57248-109-9	How to Probate an Estate in MA (2E)	$19.95	____
____	1-57248-106-4	How to Start a Business in MA (2E)	$16.95	____
____	1-57248-107-2	Landlords' Rights and Duties in MA (2E)	$19.95	____
		MICHIGAN TITLES		
____	1-57071-409-6	How to File for Divorce in MI (2E)	$19.95	____
____	1-57248-077-7	How to Make a MI Will (2E)	$12.95	____
____	1-57071-407-X	How to Start a Business in MI (2E)	$16.95	____
		MINNESOTA TITLES		
____	1-57248-039-4	How to File for Divorce in MN	$19.95	____
____	1-57248-040-8	How to Form a Simple Corporation in MN	$19.95	____
____	1-57248-037-8	How to Make a MN Will	$9.95	____
____	1-57248-038-6	How to Start a Business in MN	$16.95	____
		NEVADA TITLES		
____	1-57248-101-3	How to Form a Corporation in NV	$19.95	____
		NEW YORK TITLES		
____	1-57071-184-4	How to File for Divorce in NY	$19.95	____

Qty	ISBN	Title	Retail	Ext.
____	1-57248-105-6	How to Form a Corporation in NY	$19.95	____
____	1-57248-095-5	How to Make a NY Will (2E)	$12.95	____
____	1-57071-185-2	How to Start a Business in NY	$16.95	____
____	1-57071-187-9	How to Win in Small Claims Court in NY	$14.95	____
____	1-57071-186-0	Landlords' Rights and Duties in NY	$19.95	____
____	1-57071-188-7	New York Power of Attorney Handbook	$19.95	____
		NORTH CAROLINA TITLES		
____	1-57071-326-X	How to File for Divorce in NC (2E)	$19.95	____
____	1-57071-327-8	How to Make a NC Will (2E)	$12.95	____
____	1-57248-096-3	How to Start a Business in NC (2E)	$16.95	____
____	1-57248-091-2	Landlords' Rights & Duties in NC	$19.95	____
		OHIO TITLES		
____	1-57248-102-1	How to File for Divorce in OH	$19.95	____
		PENNSYLVANIA TITLES		
____	1-57071-177-1	How to File for Divorce in PA	$19.95	____
____	1-57248-094-7	How to Make a PA Will (2E)	$12.95	____
____	1-57248-112-9	How to Start a Business in PA (2E)	$16.95	____
____	1-57071-179-8	Landlords' Rights and Duties in PA	$19.95	____
		TEXAS TITLES		
____	1-57071-330-8	How to File for Divorce in TX (2E)	$19.95	____
____	1-57248-009-2	How to Form a Simple Corporation in TX	$19.95	____
____	1-57071-417-7	How to Make a TX Will (2E)	$12.95	____
____	1-57071-418-5	How to Probate an Estate in TX (2E)	$19.95	____
____	1-57071-365-0	How to Start a Business in TX (2E)	$16.95	____
____	1-57248-111-0	How to Win in Small Claims Court in TX (2E)	$14.95	____
____	1-57248-110-2	Landlords' Rights and Duties in TX (2E)	$19.95	____

SUBTOTAL THIS PAGE ____

SUBTOTAL PREVIOUS PAGE ____

Illinois residents add 6.75% sales tax
Florida residents add 6% state sales tax plus applicable discretionary surtax ____

Shipping— $4.00 for 1st book, $1.00 each additional ____

TOTAL ____